Lion Gate and Labyrinth

LION GATE AND LABYRINTH

BY HANS BAUMANN
TRANSLATED BY STELLA HUMPHRIES

PANTHEON BOOKS

Contents

LIST OF COLOR PLATES

Part One

SCHLIEMANN AND THE WORLD OF HOMER

Odysseus comes Home

On July 8, 1868, a small fishing boat crossed the sea between the island of Cephalonia and the isle of Ithaca, the home of Odysseus. There were two men in the boat, the fisherman and a foreign traveler. Although the wind was unfavorable, no one had been able to persuade the stranger to wait for better weather. For fourteen hours the waves kept breaking over the side of the boat but that did not dismay him, nor did he complain of hunger. His eyes were fixed on Ithaca all day, and when night fell, he held his gaze as steadily as a man who is returning home.

They had set sail that morning at six o'clock. It was an hour before midnight when they reached the little harbor of St. Spiridon. During the crossing, the foreigner, who spoke better Greek than the fisherman, plied him with questions about Odysseus, who had fought at Troy with Agamemnon and who had played a greater part than anyone else in bringing about the downfall of the city, about Achilles, and the other Achaean heroes.

"But surely you know Odysseus!"

The fisherman was at a loss. He knew a baker called Odysseus, but as for a king by that name who had lived more than three thousand years before and who had only returned to his home on Ithaca when ten long years of war and ten more years of

7

wandering were over, why no, the fisherman had never heard of him.

"You won't find anyone in our village who knows this Odysseus of yours," he assured the stranger as they made the harbor. "And there's no one here in Ithaca who has heard of him either."

But the fisherman was proved wrong immediately as it so happened. Although it was so late, a man with a donkey was standing at the quayside, as if he were waiting for someone. And when the foreigner inquired if the man could put him up for the night, the latter was clearly delighted. He introduced himself as the miller, said that it was not far to his mill, loaded the donkey with the stranger's baggage, and they set off together.

As soon as the miller learned that the visitor had come to Ithaca to dig among the ruins, it was he who brought up the name of Odysseus.

"I should know about Odysseus if anyone does," he began enthusiastically, "for my father often told me of his adventures. And he in turn had heard them from my grandfather, for the story has been handed down from father to son since the days of Odysseus' return. All these years our family has cherished his tale as its most precious possession and there isn't a house in Ithaca that has preserved it as well as we have. Odysseus was our neighbor, sir, our most illustrious neighbor."

Turning a deaf ear to all the stranger's questions, the miller went on. "Only the gods know why he should have been so sorely tested and tried before he was finally allowed to return to his home, for he was the cleverest of mortal men and it was through his cunning that Troy was finally destroyed. When the war was over, he wanted to go straight home like all the other heroes, just as Agamemnon went back to Mycenae and Nestor returned to Pylos. But storms drove his twelve ships off course to foreign shores whose very names were unknown to him. First the gales blew him northward to the Land of the Cicones. There his companions plundered the villages just as they had sacked those in

8

the plains outside Troy for the past ten years. Of course the Cicones didn't like it and slew seventy-two of them. The remainder fared better in the south, though, in the Land of the Lotus-Eaters. The spies whom Odysseus had sent ahead, did not want to return to their ships, for they had tasted the lotus fruits that made them forget their homes. Odysseus had to whip them aboard and chain them. Then the wind drove his ships westward to the island where the Cyclops lived in caves. And in the cave of the one-eyed giant Polyphemus, Odysseus accomplished an unparalleled feat.

"Polyphemus was the son of Poseidon, the god of the sea. Yet he also belonged to the race of the ungodly Cyclops, who scorned the sacred laws of hospitality and ate human flesh. As soon as Polyphemus returned to his cave that evening driving his flock of sheep before him, he discovered Odysseus, who had taken shelter there with his twelve companions, and the giant immediately devoured six of them. The others were unable to escape, for Polyphemus sealed the entrance to the cave with a large boulder.

"The next day, Odysseus offered him some of the wine he had brought with him from the Land of the Cicones. This made Polyphemus drunk and he grew merry. He asked Odysseus his name. 'Nobody,' answered Odysseus. Then the giant laughed. 'I shall eat you last, my friend.'

"But Odysseus forestalled him. As Polyphemus lay on the ground in a drunken stupor, Odysseus heated the tip of a sharpened stake in the fire that burned in the cave, and he thrust the red-hot point into the one eye of the Cyclops. With a great roar, the blinded giant leapt to his feet and groping his way to the entrance to the cave, he rolled aside the great rock that blocked it. And when the other Cyclops came running up to find out who it was who was trying to kill him, he howled, 'Nobody has blinded me! Find me Nobody!' And the Cyclops thought he was out of his mind and went away again. Odysseus, however, had

tied the giant's rams in threes, and with each of his remaining comrades clinging to the belly of the one in the middle, they managed to leave the cave unnoticed under the very nose of the sightless giant, who was feeling along the backs of the sheep with his hands.

"When the seven survivors were safely on board ship once more, Odysseus shouted taunts at Polyphemus. The latter, beside himself with fury, hurled great rocks at the ships, and when he found he could not harm them that way, he prayed to his father Poseidon to avenge him.

"From then on, it was the god of the sea who persecuted Odysseus with implacable hatred. It availed him nothing even when the friendly god of the winds tied up the adverse gales in a leather bag and gave them to Odysseus, who was yearning to get home. For his envious companions opened the bag out of idle curiosity and the tempests swooped down on the ships at once and drove them to the northernmost place, where the nights are as white as snow and where giants live who threaten the lives of everyone who comes near them. They destroyed the whole of Odysseus' fleet, except for one last ship.

"With this ship, Odysseus sailed as far as the island of the enchantress Circe. She turned his men into swine and if it had not been for Hermes, the messenger of the gods, who brought Odysseus a magic charm to counter the spell, he too would have succumbed to Circe's wiles. But he was able to force the witch

Achaean lady. Restored fresco from Tiryns, figure almost life-size

to restore his men to human shape, and the bristles fell away from them like snowflakes.

"They spent a joyous year on the island, and Circe revealed to Odysseus that before they thought of returning home, they must first travel to the portals of the underworld. When Odysseus questioned the dead on the threshold of the realm of the shades, he learned from the ghost of the seer Teiresias and from his dead mother, that he alone would survive all Poseidon's persecution, and that he would once more see the island of Ithaca, his father Laertes, his wife Penelope, and his son Telemachus.

"Then Odysseus traveled on, past the island of the Sirens, who

11

lure sailors from their course with their seductive singing. He plugged his companions' ears with wax, and then he made them bind him to the mast. So they sailed past the island unscathed and skirted the clutching whirlpool Charybdis without mishap. But the monster Scylla with her six jaws, snatched six of his men as they passed through the narrow straits. All the rest of his crew met their end on the island where the herds of the sun god grazed. Driven to madness by hunger, they laid hands on the sacred cattle. It was Zeus himself who took a flash of lightning and with it, he sank Odysseus' ship. He alone survived, drifting for nine days in the open sea, clinging to the mast. When he was washed ashore on another island, the beautiful nymph Calypso held him captive for seven long years.

"But his longing for Ithaca grew so strong, that the gods stepped in and commanded the nymph to let him go. He built himself a raft and with it he sailed for seventeen days, until Poseidon discovered him. Not far from the Land of the Phaeacians, the sea god darkened the sky and shattered the raft with mountainous waves, so that Odysseus was cast upon a foreign shore. As a peasant covers the embers of his fire with dust and ash, so did Odysseus conceal himself with foliage. That was how Nausicaä, the daughter of the King of the Phaeacians, discovered him. She gave him clothing and he washed the brine from his shoulders. After all his suffering, the Phaeacians, to whom he had related his adventures, conveyed him home to Ithaca. They carried the cunning prince ashore while he slept, and left him lying on his native soil.

"Odysseus, disguised as a beggar, made his way to his own palace. There, in the king's hall, he settled his score with the suitors who had been insolent enough to woo Penelope, his wife, and to devour his estate as if it had been their own. He alone could span his great bow, and with his son, Telemachus and two of his herdsmen by his side, the returned wanderer struck down the intruders with his arrows. The wooers fell to the ground like fruit that has hung too long on the tree and is shaken to the earth in a November gale. Then Odysseus revealed himself to his father, to his faithful wife, and to all his people, and he reigned once more in his own land. In his own Ithaca!" concluded the miller as he and the traveler reached the mill after an hour and half.

The house was not large and once they were indoors, the stranger saw that the miller had only one bed. The food was bad too, nothing but barley bread and tepid rainwater, but the foreigner had eaten nothing for twenty hours and he was grateful for both. Once he had managed to persuade the miller to take the bed, he lay down on an ironbound chest and he never slept more soundly in his life.

The next day, he climbed to the top of Mount Aetos to look for the palace of Odysseus. There he found remains of walls and towers and a dried up cistern. The heat was stifling, but the mere sight of the island where Odysseus had ruled as king, made the stranger forget both heat and thirst.

For the next three days, he got up at five o'clock in the morning, and taking a few workmen with him, he climbed up the hill to probe the site where Odysseus had had his palace. He dug in vain for the remains of the olive tree around which Odysseus had built his sleeping chamber, but he did find a small burial ground containing ash-filled urns. Then he came upon the rocky path that led downhill from the citadel to Laertes' farm, where Odysseus had met his father in the garden. The stranger found a group of villagers gathered there, and since they received him kindly he read aloud to them the passage from Homer's *Odyssey* which describes the reunion of Odysseus and his father. It tells how the long-suffering hero, to test the gray-haired old man, first pretended that he was a seaman from Crete, but at last, disclosed his identity.

His listeners were moved to tears and they embraced the stranger in Laertes' field as if it were he who had come home after years of wandering, and carried him off in triumph to the village.

The next day, the stranger explored the southern part of the island and here he came upon a remote farmstead. He was about to ask for a drink of water, when four dogs rushed out at him. He raised his stick and this enraged the dogs. Fortunately, he remembered a passage from the *Odyssey*, which runs as follows: "The noisy dogs suddenly caught sight of Odysseus and flew at him, barking loudly. He had the presence of mind to sit down and drop his staff."

The stranger followed his example, and the dogs were content to bar his path and stand around him, bristling and snarling, until their owner came out to see what was wrong. The visitor reproached him for having *four* dogs, but the farmer told him almost angrily: "We have kept four dogs on this farm since the days of Odysseus." This explanation pacified the stranger, but the farmer insisted on offering him grapes and peaches and lavishing such hospitality on him that even the dogs became friendly. At last the farmer asked the stranger where he came from.

"From Cephalonia," replied the stranger.

Sprawling dog on lid of green steatite jar. Early Minoan, c. 2400 B.C. I. of Mochlos, eastern Crete

"But you're not from those parts," said the Greek. "Where is your home?"

At that, the stranger grew thoughtful.

"But don't you know where your home is?" persisted the farmer, surprised.

"The answer is not as simple as you think," he said. "For the last two years, I have been in France. Before that I was in India, China, and Japan. And before that, I lived in Russia. I have been in the United States, Sweden, Italy, Egypt . . ."

"You are indeed an Odysseus," said the farmer. "How long have you been traveling?"

"Thirty years. But now I am here in Greece, where I always longed to be."

"Your journey has lasted three times as long as that of Odysseus," said the farmer. "Tell me though, who are you?"

"My name is Schliemann," answered the stranger. "I come from Ankershagen, in Germany."

Schliemann's Odyssey to Ithaca

He was fourteen years old when he left Ankershagen. His father, a parson who had been deprived of his living, could no longer pay the boy's school tuition. Schliemann was devoted to him all his life. It was through his father that he first heard of Troy, of Achilles and Odysseus, of Helen, Agamemnon, Hector and Paris, for he had given him a children's "History of the World" as a present, and one of the pictures in it showed Troy in flames. The child, Heinrich, had marveled at the massive walls of Troy.

"Were they really as thick as they are in the picture?" he asked.

"No doubt of it," said his father.

"Then there must be a lot of them left still," said Heinrich.

"But no one knows where Troy is," explained his father.

"Then I shall go and look for it one day," declared the child.

When he made that resolution, he was eight years old. That Christmas, in rather shaky Latin, he wrote the history of the Trojan War for his father.

Four years later, he found himself an apprentice in a shop that reeked of herring, tallow candles and spirits. His working day started at five in the morning and finished at eleven at night. Wood shavings clung to his jacket and breeches. And amidst all of this, he dreamed of becoming a rich man. He dreamed of the United States where, so they said, the streets were paved with gold. But there was no place for his Trojan reveries during those dark years. Then one day, a miller came into the shop. He was somewhat tipsy and he began to recite poetry in a language that Heinrich had never heard before, an extract from a long epic.

Schliemann asked him what it was. "It's a poem by Homer," replied the man. "The story of the Trojan War. In Greek," he added proudly. As the boy bought him a glass of brandy out of his own pocket, the miller quoted another passage from the *Iliad*.

Opposite: Entrance to the 'Treasury of Atreus', Mycenae

Then the yearning for Troy gripped the boy once more, but he could see no way of escaping from the shop, which had become his prison. At last a barrel of chicory came to his aid.

It was too heavy for him and as he lifted it, he collapsed and began to spit blood. That was the end of dragging sacks of potatoes, of lifting crates and vats. The shopkeeper dismissed him because he was too weak. With thirty thalers in his pocket, Heinrich Schliemann set off on foot for Hamburg. There, he taught himself bookkeeping by the "Schwanbeck System" in a single week. He was thrilled by the city's towers and even more by the port, where ships docked that sailed the whole world. He outfitted himself for a long voyage. To do this, he sold his wrist watch, and with the money, he went to an old clothes' dealer and bought two shirts, a coat, a pair of trousers, a mattress and a woolen blanket with so many patches that it looked like a map. On November 28, 1841, he set off for Venezuela as cabin boy on the brig *Dorothea*. In his spare time, he started learning Spanish.

On December 1, a storm arose which increased in force each day. The thermometer fell to six degrees below zero and snow storms turned the day into darkness. On December 11, the main topgallant sail broke away and a few days later, the storm sail mast snapped. Daylight was smothered in thick clouds. Only once did the dense wall divide and between the mountainous waves, the boy caught glimpse of the dancing sun. The drag anchor had long since been dropped and now the hawsers snapped. At midnight, the captain bellowed, "The ship's sinking!"

Schliemann was wearing only a few rags. Like all the others on board he had been battered and bruised. Three of his front teeth were broken. His terror made him see sharks lurking in the water. The ship's bell had not finished sounding the alarm when two of the lifeboats were shattered to pieces before they could even be launched. Only the boat astern reached the water safely.

At that moment, the ship went down. Schliemann clung to an empty cask and drifted along until the lifeboat picked him up.

It carried fourteen men for two days through the gale before it ran aground on the sands of Texel, an island off the Dutch coast. A peasant there gave Schliemann a blanket, a pair of trousers, wooden shoes and a hat.

The next day, the chest he had had on board was washed ashore; he was the only person who had such amazing luck. That dark monster, the sea, had not kept him in its clutches and had even spewed up his worldly goods onto dry land. The others were envious and called him a Jonah, but on that day, he determined never to give in, no matter what blows fate held in store for him.

The shipwrecked survivors were offered their passage back to Germany but Schliemann refused and decided to seek his fortune in Holland instead. He wanted to be a merchant, rich and independent, so that one day, he could look for Troy and dig up the remains of the city.

He went to Amsterdam and from his first day there, he began to study languages. Wherever he could, whenever his duties as an errand boy allowed him the time, standing at the counter of the post office, in the rain, in waiting rooms, he pulled a book from his pocket and began learning words and sentences by heart. He never missed a sermon at the English church and in six months' time, he was speaking English as well as he spoke German. During the next six months, he learned French. In the years that followed, he added three more languages in addition to Dutch—Italian, Portuguese, and Spanish.

On March 1, 1844, he was given a post in the trading firm of Schröder's, at a yearly salary of six hundred gulden. By then, he could write letters in seven languages, and he proved himself so capable that after one month, his salary was raised to one thousand gulden.

Since Schröder's had business dealings with Russia, Schliemann volunteered to learn Russian in six weeks. And he did it, too. With the aid of a grammar, a dictionary, and a Russian transla-

Ship in a storm.
Flattened cylinder, Knossos

tion of the *Adventures of Telemachus,* he acquired the necessary vocabulary. Since there was no teacher of Russian in the whole of Amsterdam, Schliemann hired an audience of one to whom he could repeat his lessons. For the sum of one gulden a day, an old Jew who knew not a single word of this difficult language, sat and listened for six weeks, as the young man from Mecklenburg declaimed aloud and drank innumerable cups of tea. At the end of the six weeks, Schliemann wrote his first letter in Russian to Vassili Plotnikov, the London agent of a big indigo firm from Moscow. There was not a single mistake in it.

Businessmen from Russia were quick to notice this highly gifted young man. A man from St. Petersburg offered to set up a new firm, Zhivago and Schliemann, and make him a partner. Then Schröder's sent him to Russia as their representative.

Two years later, Schliemann had his own business and capital in the bargain. Soon he was a wholesaler and before long, he was given hereditary, honorary Russian citizenship. He was also made a director of the Imperial State Bank at St. Petersburg. To achieve all this, however, he never spared himself. He made long journeys by sleigh through the frozen countryside. Often he was ill. Once his life hung in the balance.

He was twenty-eight years old when he received news that his brother Ludwig had died in California. He read it in a newspaper clipping which stated that a certain Louis Schliemann had left a large fortune. This was reason enough for Heinrich Schliemann to set off at once for the new El Dorado. But the *Atlantic* on which he was sailing, ran into a storm that wrecked the steering gear. When the engines failed, too, the captain rigged up sails that "looked like pocket handkerchiefs." The hurricane drove the ship back to Europe. It was on the *Africa* that Schliemann reached New York three weeks later. When he learned that his brother had died intestate, instead of wasting time with legal proceedings, he went out west himself, to the place where Ludwig had made his fortune. Armed with a revolver and a dagger, he first had to cross the jungle, like many another goldseeker. He saw "butterflies as big as doves" and much misery as well. On the nights of June 4 and 5, 1851, he escaped from the great fire of San Francisco, in which several foreigners were lynched as arsonists. Out west, he founded a bank for transactions in gold dust. He contracted yellow fever and came back via Panama, where for days on end he had to subsist on the iguanas he caught. Eventually he returned to Europe with gangrene in one leg. He was thirty years of age; he had doubled his fortune in the United States; and he went back to St. Petersburg once more.

The following year he married a Russian woman who was not at all the right wife for him. Nevertheless, Fate overwhelmed him with worldly wealth. When a big fire in Memel swept through the warehouse area and Schliemann was faced with the total loss of all his property there, it turned out that his goods were stored in the only warehouse at the docks which had not been burned to the ground.

He went on learning languages, Swedish, Danish, Norwegian, Polish and Slovene. And in 1855, when his son was born, he learned both modern Greek and the language of Homer, which meant more to him than any other. On a journey through Italy and Egypt, he added Latin, Arabic and Persian to the list.

For three more years, he served Hermes, the god of merchants and thieves. By then, his fortune was so vast that he could take the biggest step in his career. At the age of forty, he gave up all his business enterprises so that he could devote himself to the task he had set his mind on as a child. He was going to excavate the walls of Troy.

But he was still not quite ready to begin. Before that, he wished to travel farther afield, through three continents. For in spite of his rise from rags to riches, in spite of his knowledge of languages which opened so many doors to him, he was not a happy man. There was no one who understood him. In one letter, he said he was afraid he would never be anything but a dilettante. "My scribblings collapse about me like a house without foundations," he wrote.

Schliemann resolved to study but first he decided to go around the world and inspect some famous ruins. His first destination was Carthage and then he paid his second visit to the Pyramids. From there he went on to Ceylon and through northern India to

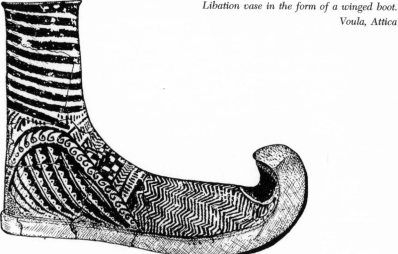

Libation vase in the form of a winged boot.
Voula, Attica

the Himalayas. After visiting Java, where he spent several happy days, he arrived in China, the "Middle Kingdom" as the Chinese themselves call it, which he had been looking forward to with great anticipation. But much in China displeased and even disgusted him. He did not like the smells, the dust and the dirty inns, the beggars and the rag collectors. He was revolted by the decapitated heads and the decaying temples, and he disliked the unfamiliar food and traveling in rickshaws.

Two encounters, however, were of decisive importance for him. He met an Englishman named Robert Thomas, who had mastered Russian, German, Swedish, French, Spanish, Portuguese, Italian, Japanese and Chinese in a remarkably short time. Thomas was a man who was as cultured as he was modest, and he proved extremely helpful to the exuberant German globe-trotter in every possible way.

From Peking, Schliemann made an unusual expedition. Because no one else would go with him, he set out alone. He traveled in an uncomfortable cart, riding on the shaft most of the way, making for the Great Wall of China. This mightiest of all human constructions was built in obedience to the will of the "Son of Heaven," and stretches through desert and mountain for more than 1,500 miles.

It was an exciting moment for Schliemann as he scaled the wall. In his imagination, he could see it stormed by assault forces and defended by the Chinese. He took exact measurements and broke off a piece of the stone. To everyone's amusement, when he returned to Peking, he was carrying it on his back. Later, in his first book, he declared that he had dreamt of the walls of Troy and Mycenae by the Great Wall of China.

Japan, his next goal, captivated him. He inspected public buildings and baths, he admired the charm of Japanese women, he saw the usurper Emperor riding past in a great procession, and observed with horror that the parade passed over the bodies of three of His Majesty's slain enemies.

Next, he crossed the Pacific and spent the voyage writing his first book, his impressions of China and Japan. He landed in the United States at San Francisco, visited Nicaragua and Mexico and finally settled in Paris to study archaeology at the Sorbonne. In the spring of 1868, he went back to the United States and called on the President. He also visited Negro schools and transacted some private business. On his return to Paris, he was greeted by the news of the sudden death of his cousin Sophie, to whom he had been greatly attached. It was this abrupt loss that brought him to a sense of urgency. Now was the time to begin his quest for Troy seriously.

After thirty years of drifting, he started out for Greece. Traveling by way of Naples and Corfu, he landed on Ithaca on July 8, 1868 from a fishing boat—a genius whose wife thought he was insane, a homeless wanderer, yearning for a home of his own. On the island of Odysseus, for the first time, he stepped ashore, into the world for which he was born.

From Ithaca, he went on to Mycenae, the stronghold of Agamemnon, Prince of the Achaeans who had led the expedition

The 'Treasury of Atreus'. Bottom Left: Ground plan. Above: Linear section, corresponding to the line A–B. Lower right: Cross section, corresponding to the line C–D. The domed chamber is concealed within the hill. The lintel is made of two blocks, the inner one weighing approx. 100 tons.

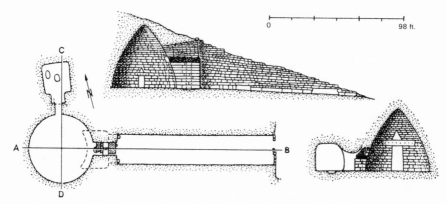

against Troy. There were still footpads and brigands roaming the mountains of Greece in Schliemann's day and it was not uncommon for travelers to be waylaid and lose all their money, sometimes even their lives. When Schliemann set off for Mycenae from the small town of Argos, the worried lieutenant in charge of the garrison insisted on giving him two soldiers as a bodyguard, but on questioning these men, Schliemann discovered that the name of Mycenae meant nothing at all to them. So he left them behind in the village at the foot of the hill where the citadel stands. Instead, he took with him a boy who said that he knew where "The Palace of Agamemnon" lay, and also "The Treasury of Atreus" and other ruins. With the *Iliad* in his hand, Schliemann climbed the broad mound to the fortress which is dominated by two bare mountain peaks, one on either side.

From a distance he caught sight of the walls with their Cyclopean blocks of stone. He explored the whole site and took measurements. Then he stood and gazed for a long time at a half ruined gateway, the very sight of which took his breath away.

Above the lintel, which is a granite slab weighing twenty tons, stands a pair of stone lions, rampant and facing one another. Their heads are missing, and yet their bodies seem alive. With a pillar between them, they stand guard over the entrance to Agamemnon's fortress.

Schliemann kept his eyes open for tombs, but there was no sign of them anywhere. The boy then took him to "The Treasury of Atreus" which lies concealed in the hillside just a few hundred yards from the Lion Gate. A passage some one hundred sixty-five feet long with walls thirty-three feet high leads to the entrance gateway.

Schliemann entered the lofty room, which is shaped like a beehive and is built of sheer freestone blocks. He noticed at once that behind it was another room, a square chamber roughly hewn out of the rock. The narrow communicating doorway allowed little light to enter, so inside this bare dungeon it was as dark and inhospitable as a cave.

To his annoyance, Schliemann discovered that he had no matches in his pocket. He asked the boy to bring back some from the village, but he assured him that there were none there. However, when Schliemann promised him half a drachma for three matches and confirmed the offer with an oath on Agamemnon, the boy raced down to the village and soon returned with a bundle of firewood and ten matches. Schliemann made a fire in the inner chamber. Bats flew up from every corner, startled by the firelight. But in spite of all his searching, Schliemann discovered nothing remarkable. Outside the Treasury, however, he noticed fragments of pottery and copper nails.

In the glow of sunset, the walls of Mycenae shone like gold. The man and the boy returned to the two soldiers who had fallen asleep under a tree. They did not wake up until Schliemann sprinkled their faces with water. After a ride of a few hours, they were back in Argos again, not far from the coast, their starting point.

Schliemann was determined to come back again one day and dig in Mycenae. It is mentioned many times in the *Iliad* and the *Odyssey*. "Mycenae, rich in gold," is what Homer calls it.

Only one place had an even more impressive ring in Homer's works and that was Troy itself. Now that Schliemann had visited the strongholds of Agamemnon and Odysseus, he wanted to set forth like the Achaeans before him and conquer Troy—or what was left of it.

Schliemann was convinced that the Trojan War had really taken place, just as Homer had described it. In his eyes, Achilles and Hector, Castor and Pollux, Andromache and Helen were not mythical figures but men and women who had actually lived and suffered the horrors of a deadly struggle that lasted for ten years. Nor were the events any less credible for Schliemann just because the gods were supposed to be the cause of it all and were said to have taken part in the battles. Paris, the Trojan Prince, had certainly abducted Helen from Sparta. The Achaean fleet really had set sail for Troy to win back the most beautiful woman on earth and to have their revenge. The quarrel between Achilles and Agamemnon, the death of Patroclus and of the noble Hector, the wooden horse of Odysseus and the burning of Troy were facts for Schliemann. They were as indisputable as his own birth and his adventures on four continents.

In 1868, he started for the Troad, which is the northeasternmost point in Asia Minor, in order to search for the city of Troy on a hill near the Dardanelles. He had complete confidence in both of Homer's epics. For him, the key to success lay in the text of the *Iliad* and the *Odyssey*.

Swans on a Mycenean vase. Argos

In Search of Troy

The victorious Achaeans had left Troy a heap of ruins. But even if the day had come when "sacred Ilium" had disappeared without a trace, it had been preserved vividly in folk memory as the most famous city of all time.

The Persian king Xerxes had sacrificed a thousand oxen on the hill of Troy before he set out on his expedition to the west, to avenge Priam and his people on the Greeks. Alexander had begun his Indian campaign by running a lap of honor around the grave of Achilles. Pompey, who traced his ancestry through the most ancient kings of Rome back to the Trojan hero Aeneas, had pierced the oak thicket that concealed the ruins of Troy and he resolved to build the capital of the world on the spot. Constantine wanted to do the same. Emperors, fools, and admirers all made pilgrimages to the place where Hector had slain Patroclus and Achilles had killed Hector. Greeks and Romans tried to restore the prehistoric city to a new glory, but without success. When the Anglo-Saxon chronicler, Seawulf, sailed along the coast of the Troad in about 1100 A.D., he saw nothing but ruins, "strewn for miles." Two hundred years later, that mysterious gentleman, Sir John Mandeville, reported that there was not the slightest trace of Troy left. The city lapsed into a theme for poets and painters, a mere subject for generations of schoolboys to whom Homer's poems were nothing more than required reading.

The Turks sealed off Troy from Europe and only a handful of bold adventurers succeeded in finding their way there. In 1552, a French diplomat called Bellon who had studied at Wittenberg visited the site, and an Italian, Pietro della Valle, drank "Trojan water" from a tank in Alexandria, a town in Asia Minor. In the year 1676, two travelers got through, Jacques Spon and George Wheler, but they were all looking in the wrong place. Only George Sandys, Lady Mary Wortley Montague, and the explorer

Richard Pococke were put on the right track by local inhabitants. Shepherds and peasants occasionally made finds on the hill of Hissarlik, which suggested that the place had a venerable history.

That was one hundred and fifty years before Schliemann. In 1822, an archaeologist named Maclaren said that he believed Troy lay buried in the hill of Hissarlik. The German scholar Moltke, agreed with him. An Austrian, von Hahn, even dug there for a few days, after Turkish looters had extracted a considerable treasure of silver coins from the mound. These coins were approximately two thousand years old. But most people looked for Troy elsewhere. They believed that Homer's city lay within the hill of Bunarbashi, which lies about six miles to the south. Moltke, for one, thought that this hill was the more likely of the two and so for that matter, did the British Admiralty, because it is a commanding site and suitable for a fortress. Everyone who gave any thought at all to the location of Troy concluded that the case for Bunarbashi was overwhelming. In any event, there were very few who seriously believed that Homer's Troy had ever really existed.

In the year 1868, when Schliemann left Mycenae for his first visit to Troy, there was only one person apart from the "Odysseus from Ankershagen" who had faith in it, and that was an Englishman, Frank Calvert. He was the American consul for the Dardanelles, and he had lived in the Troad since 1859. Inspired by Homer, he had scoured the countryside, searching for the remains of Troy. He found a number of mounds that suggested ancient settlements, and the hill of Hissarlik seemed more promising to Calvert than that of Bunarbashi. Hissarlik, a Turkish word, gave a clue. It means 'a small fortress'. In 1860, Calvert had scratched at the surface of the mound, the eastern half of which he had actually bought, but he did not have the money for any extensive excavation. He kept trying to interest the British Museum in the site, as well as an archaeological society, but with little success. When then, in August 1868, a man appeared on the scene who was determined to find Troy, with money

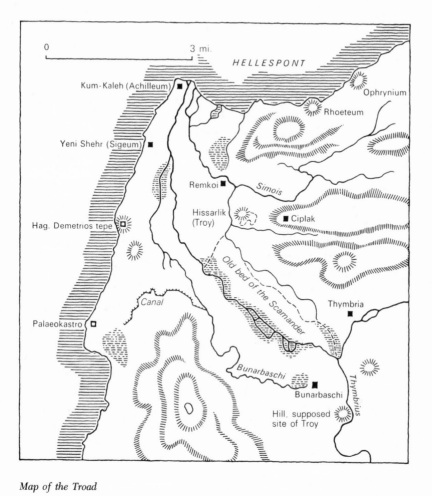

Map of the Troad

enough to have the mound literally removed if necessary, no one
was more delighted than Frank Calvert.

Admittedly, Schliemann's first choice had been Bunarbashi too.
There he found a village of miserable huts, so full of fleas and
filth that he was obliged to sleep out of doors at night, in the

29

open fields. On three scorching days, he dug thirty test pits in the hill, but neither potsherds nor the stone blocks of Trojan walls came to light.

Bunarbashi lies about nine miles from the place where the Greeks most probably berthed their ships during the siege. The hill of Hissarlik, on the other hand, is much nearer, about three miles away. Schliemann opened the *Iliad* and he calculated that if Troy had really been located on the hill of Bunarbashi, the Achaeans must have covered fifty-two miles in nine hours of fighting, back and forth between the beach and Troy. The Achaeans carried shields that protected them from top to toe. They also had heavy armor, spears and swords, which Homer described in great detail. Even for powerful heroes so equipped, it would have been impossible for them to cover that distance in a day and engage in battle too. But one third of that distance (or roughly eighteen miles) was possible even for ordinary fighting men. This seemed a conclusive argument for Hissarlik, but even so Schliemann was not quite satisfied.

He reread carefully the passage in which Homer describes Achilles' terrible pursuit of Hector around the walls of Troy. Apollo had lured Achilles to the bank of the Scamander, almost to the two springs which are its source, one of which runs warm and the other cold. As soon as Achilles saw Hector standing before the Scaean Gate, he launched his attack. Unnerved by the awe-inspiring radiance of Achilles' armor, Hector took to flight. The two heroes circled the walls of the city three times, past the hill with the fig tree and the two springs, "and all the gods watched." Schliemann wanted to see if it could be done, so he set off at a very fast run, just as Homer described it. He started from the Scamander, making a beeline for the two springs, and then he veered southeast following a ravine that divides the mound from the rocks. Stubbornly finding out for himself, Schliemann had a wearying hour's run around to the southwest side of the hill, where he came to a sheer drop. This cliff face was four hundred ninety five feet high, and he slithered down it backward on all fours, and into the gully below. By this time, he was convinced that no one with human lungs and human feet could have circled the hill of Bunarbashi three times and then gone on to fight a duel to the death. Schliemann devoured the only food he carried with him, a hunk of barley bread. To quench his thirst, he drank water from the Scamander, sinking his arms to the elbows in mud.

Then he recalled the two springs. According to Homer: "In one of these, the water comes up hot; steam rises from it . . . but the other even in summer, gushes up as cold as hail or freezing snow." Schliemann plunged a thermometer into each of them. They both registered the same temperature, 49.5° F. Then he made a further discovery. In a radius of $\frac{3}{10}$ of a mile, he found spring after spring, thirty-four in all! His companion, a man from the village, showed him another six and told him that in Turkish, the place was called Kirk Gios, which means roughly "Forty Eyes." Schliemann ruled out Bunarbashi there and then for good.

On August 14, he rode out to the hill of Hissarlik on which Frank Calvert had pinned such high hopes, arriving at ten o'clock in the morning. Calvert showed him potsherds and the remains of pillars that he had found during his digging. It was he too, who told Schliemann that there must be not one Troy, but several cities concealed within the mound, each built upon the ruins of its predecessor. He must be prepared to excavate a number of strata.

Schliemann ascertained that the hill top formed a flat rectangle about seven hundred thirty seven feet by six hundred fifty six. He had imagined that Ilium was a much mightier city, but all the same, he did not doubt that Calvert was right. Presumably the remains of the "populous city" lay on the bedrock of the mound itself and in the earth around it. That was why he decided to remove any later buildings he happened to find over a wide area, in order to uncover the palaces and temples of Homeric Troy which, he assumed, lay in the deepest stratum of all.

But there was still a point of detail that troubled Schliemann greatly. There was no sign anywhere of the two springs. He asked Calvert about them and he gave Schliemann a possible explanation for their absence. In a region which is always liable to earthquakes, springs could appear and disappear from one day to the next, he told him. Calvert had seen this happen with his own eyes only three years before, when the hot springs of Tongla had simply vanished during an earthquake. As far back as people could remember, the plains of Troy had been considered seismic territory.

Schliemann was satisfied at last. For six days he had eaten nothing but barley bread and drunk water from the river. Now he visited a village near the sea and ordered a chicken at an inn. They had to catch the bird first, though, and as Schliemann watched, it began to screech so pitifully that it would have melted a heart of stone. Thereupon Schliemann paid for the chicken but spared its life. He contented himself with eggs and bread and washed them down with wine. For the night, he had intended

Plan of Troy. Cross-section north-south (cf. ground-plan, p. 85). F Bed-rock; I Troy I; II Troy II; IV Troy IV, surface level; VI Troy VI (shaded); VII Troy VII, surface level; H Talus; E The Plain of Troy; R Height of later Roman city, which was built on the mound with the top 'sliced off'.

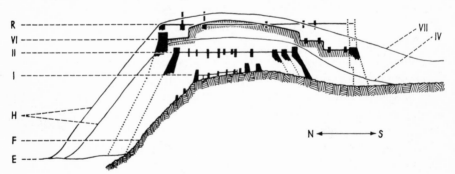

Opposite: (Above) Bronze blade of dagger, with three lions. Mycenae
(Below) The 'Nile Dagger', with leopards and wild ducks. Mycenae

to sleep on the roof of the stable, for the house was swarming with vermin, but when a cloud of fleas attacked him on the roof, he spent the rest of the night in the open field. Ever since he arrived in the Troad he had become used to this.

The next day, Schliemann went back to Constantinople and there he alarmed Frank Calvert by announcing his intention to start digging at once. Calvert advised him strongly against it. He knew how easy it was to be carried away by enthusiasm if one allowed it free rein. He had studied archaeology thoroughly and he could judge how arduous and prolonged an undertaking the excavation of Troy was going to be. Therefore he proposed to Schliemann that he should first apply for a *firman* or permit from the Turkish authorities, that they should then prepare everything in advance and wait until the spring, which would be a more favorable time of year to begin excavating.

Frank Calvert gave his advice most unselfishly. Half the hill belonged to him and he placed it at Schliemann's disposal. He also promised to persuade the owner to sell the other half of the mound. Anyone else would probably have tried to thwart the excavation of Troy.

From Constantinople, Schliemann went to Paris. In Paris he wrote his second book which he completed within a few weeks, *Ithaca, the Peloponnese and Troy;* first in English and then in German. On many of its pages the book sounds as dry as a corporation's annual report, but here and there there are flashes of ideas which reveal the daring spirit of the explorer.

The book was Schliemann's first step on the way to fame. He was offered membership in the Paris Archaeological Society on the strength of it, and it was this book that moved The University of Rostock to give him a doctorate for the story of his life, written in classical Greek. This was an honor that Schliemann valued more than his millions.

He never stopped thinking about Troy but Calvert had still been unable to obtain the excavation permit for him. Schliemann bombarded him with letters which were full of questions. What medicines should he bring with him, what digging equipment, what weapons and what kind of headgear? Would Greeks or Turks be more suitable for the work, and what were his expenses likely to be? Calvert answered the interminable list patiently, point by point. He made objections when they seemed called for, corrected Schliemann's calculations and advised him like an old friend. Since he had been present at the excavation of Nineveh, he could say with authority what was absolutely indispensable and what would also be useful. In fact, he was consulted on everything from measuring instruments to the best kind of tea to take.

Schliemann had to go to the United States once more to settle his personal affairs. In a street car in New York, he had a noteworthy experience. An eight year old boy was moving along the aisle, trying to sell some little books. "Two cents each!" he called aloud, but he stopped by the side of each passenger in turn and whispered privately, "Three for five cents to you, sir, as a special favor!" Schliemann was so impressed by this business acumen that he handed the boy a dollar. The boy refused to take it as a gift. "I'm not a beggar," he protested, "but I'll take the dollar if you'll buy sixty books from me." This Schliemann did and he told the boy who was trying to support a fatherless family by his efforts, that he foresaw a shining future for him.

In the United States, Schliemann dissolved his unhappy marriage to the Russian woman who had never understood him. Then he wrote to a Theokletos Vimpos, an old friend who had taught him Greek in St. Petersburg and who was now the Archbishop of Athens. He asked the priest to find him a Greek wife, someone he could marry with an easy mind. And in Colonus, the birthplace of Sophocles, the archbishop found a girl who was "as beautiful as Helen." Schliemann went to see her parents, then got the girl to answer three test questions and married her without delay.

Now he had a helpmate for his excavation projects. There was no longer any obstacle to his making a start on digging up Troy, nothing that is, except that the Turkish Government still refused to grant him a permit, and there was also uncertainty as to whether or not the owner of the western half of the hill of Hissarlik would agree to sell it.

Schliemann used this breathing space to explore the eastern Mediterranean. Accompanied by one sailor who obviously knew less than he should have about navigation, he sailed from island to island. They put in at the granite island of Delos on which Apollo was born; at Paros that had provided the marble for the most beautiful temple in Greece; and Naxos, the island of Dionysius. Then the boat ran into a gale and tossed about for four days until it was finally wrecked on the coast of the island of Santorin.

It was not the first time that Schliemann had suffered an ordeal by storm. But shipwreck had always been followed by a lucky turn of events for him, so he accepted his misfortune and his rescue alike with equanimity. He was thrilled by the multi-colored volcanic rocks of Santorin which tower six hundred fifty-six feet above sea level. He bought Stone Age vessels from the islanders and he went back to Athens to get ready for the ex-

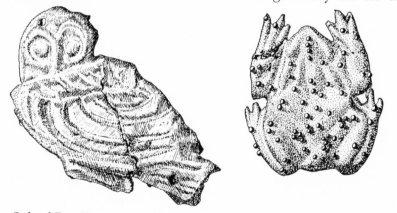

Owl and Frog. Mycenean granulated golden ornaments. Kakovatos, nr. Pylos

pedition to Troy, together with Sophia. He intended to get his hands on the western half of the hill of Hissarlik—at any price.

This land belonged to two Turkish farmers from Kum-Kaleh, a nearby village, who used the hill as pastureland for sheep. In order to be able to strike a bargain with them, Schliemann learned Turkish—in eighteen days.

His workmen meanwhile were digging up freestone blocks. The owners came running to protest. Schliemann tried to arouse their enthusiasm for Homer, but the farmers were only interested in the masonry. And when Schliemann offered them forty francs, and said he would have no objection if they used the stone to build themselves a small bridge, they let themselves be persuaded. In the end, they came to terms on a purchase price of one thousand francs. Then Savfet Pasha, the Turkish Minister of Education got wind of the affair. With great secrecy, he hastily intervened and bought the other half of the hill for six hundred francs. Schliemann felt he had been cheated and began his fight for the permit which would finally make it possible for him to dig at Hissarlik legally and unmolested.

He wrote letter after letter. With dogged persistence, he approached anyone he believed might have some influence, pestering ministers and ambassadors. He managed to enter Paris while it was besieged, with a false passport made out in the name of one Postmaster Klein from Lagny, because he was concerned about his property there. On several occasions, he was in danger of being shot as a spy.

It took a whole year before he had the official excavation permit in his hands. It contained a condition that half of all his finds must be handed over to the Turkish government.

In a trial dig, the first article that Schliemann extracted from "the embers of Troy" was a silver coin. He took it as a good omen. One cannot divide a coin in two without destroying its value. He hoped for more finds of the same kind, where division would be just as obviously ruled out in advance.

Schliemann excavates Troy

On October 11, 1871, Schliemann began demolishing the mound of Hissarlik. He had eight workmen and eight wheelbarrows, which he had brought back with him from France. From the moment they started digging, Sophia, his young wife, was his indispensable second in command. Savfet Pasha, the Minister, had sent an observer to keep an eye on things for the Turkish government.

On the following day, the number of men at work had already risen to thirty-five and on October 13, Schliemann was able to increase it to seventy-four. Eventually there were on an average one hundred people at work on the site.

A Greek named Yannakis paid their wages. He was also Schliemann's cook and personal bodyguard, and he knew all the local dialects. Schliemann counted on him more than on anyone else and even called him by his proper name. For all the others he found new names, according to how their appearance happened to strike him. If they looked rather pious, he called them Monk or Dervish. The scholarly or military ones found themselves dubbed Doctor, Schoolmaster or Corporal, and the workmen immediately followed suit, even among themselves. Schliemann used to say that was how he came to have so many men of learning about him who could neither read nor write.

He was very strict in seeing that the work went on without interruption. When he saw how much time was lost by smoking, he forbade it. The men downed tools and the few blacklegs were stoned by the others. But Schliemann was not to be intimidated and started recruiting new hands. Whereupon the old ones bowed to the inevitable and went on with their digging twice as energetically as before.

Every find was rewarded by a small coin, every forgery was punished by a fine of eight times the amount.

At first they had only wooden hoes and spades at their disposal. The rubble was carted away in fifty baskets by porters, which was time-consuming. Schliemann got oxcarts instead and eventually he replaced these by something better still. In the end, the considerable quantities of rubble were carted away in trucks along railroad tracks.

A friend from England obtained some excellent metal picks and spades for him with which the earth and debris could be broken up more easily, and sixty strong wheelbarrows arrived with the despatch from London. There was great rejoicing at this unexpected gift.

Every day, work began before sunrise. The longest working day lasted from quarter to five until quarter past seven in the evening, or fourteen and a half hours in all.

For Sophia and himself, Schliemann built a little wooden cabin on the hill. He set up a shop for the workmen, in which they could buy bread and general stores. Water had to be fetched from a spring a quarter of a mile away.

During the first three days of the 'dig' there was a constant threat to the lives of all those working there. They were disturbing the hill after a sleep that had lasted for centuries and it took its revenge. Hundreds of little brown poisonous snakes appeared, and they had to be killed. They are called *antelion,* which means that when they bite, the victim has only until sunset to live. In one of his first reports on the excavation, Schliemann paid tribute to the thousands of storks that pursued these snakes during the spring and summer in the low-lying plains around Troy. In his opinion, they alone made the Troad fit for human habitation.

Schliemann was shocked by the misery he saw in the neighboring villages. He, who could hardly bear the sight of blood, visited the sick in the workmen's huts and gave them medicine. Once a girl who was covered with ulcers was brought to him. Several times a day, she almost choked to death from coughing.

Schliemann prescribed sea baths for her and made her do exercises to relieve her breathing. Two weeks later, the girl walked from her village to Hissarlik, a journey of three hours on foot, and kissed Schliemann's shoes. The sea bathing had cured her.

Wherever this strange foreigner appeared, admiring glances followed him. It was said of him that he was a man to move mountains, and that was literally what he proposed to do.

Before Schliemann, no one had ever attempted to dig out a whole city from the earth and there was no technique of any kind laid down for a project like this.

Schliemann dug test pits which pierced the upper strata over the whole site. When the edge of a well was exposed, he had the shaft cleared immediately and from this well, galleries were driven into the lowest stratum. Broken handmade pottery, still unpainted, came to light, and jugs with faces on them and a goblet with two handles, which fitted the description of such a cup in the *Iliad*. This completely convinced Schliemann that Homer's Troy could lie only in the lowest stratum. There was nothing to do but dig right down to bedrock. A broad trench was dug, running from north to south right through the mound. And in spite of the continuous gales and cloudbursts, in spite of mosquitoes, malaria and shortage of water, in spite of August heat and February frost that froze the water to ice inside their log cabin, in spite of lice, fleas and snakes and the incessant

Stone axes. Troy

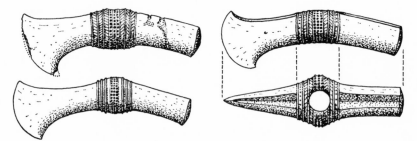

screeching of innumerable owls, in spite of insubordination among the workmen and the petty attitude of the authorities, approximately nine million cubic feet of earth and rubble was removed in the next two and a half years.

At last, a deep trench as much as two hundred and fifty feet wide in some places, pierced the hill of Hissarlik. Twenty shafts were sunk so that the remaining parts of the mound could be probed. Photidas, a Greek mining engineer who had worked in Australia, was responsible for the surveying. There came to light vessels, shells and spinning whorls, millstones and sharks' bones, vast quantities of stone tools made of black diorite, but above all, there were blocks of stone.

Clearing these blocks out of the way was one of their constant problems. On November 24, it took sixty five men a good three hours to shift one colossal doorsill, even with the use of ropes and rollers. Everything that stood in the way of access to rock bottom had to yield. According to a calculation made by a civil engineer named Laurent in April 1872, as much as six hundred fifty cubic yards of rubble were carted away on good days. With so much activity, it was inevitable that some of the pottery and earthenware figures got broken. The deeper the trenches were dug, the greater was the danger for the men digging. Stones came rolling down and often the workmen had to jump aside very quickly to save themselves.

Schliemann had the site terraced and supporting walls were built. One day, when six workmen in the charge of Photidas were shoring up a wall with props, it suddenly caved in. It was a miracle that they were all rescued.

About June 18, 1872, an earthwork collapsed burying Photidas and one of the workmen beneath it. They had been trying to bore a gallery through the earthwork, lining it with blocks of wood and thick planks as they went. Now two thousand six hundred fifty nine cubic feet of earth and stone came crashing down on them. At the greatest danger to their own lives, Schliemann and a few helpers used pocket knives to cut their way through and they found that the timber lining had stood up to the pressure of the avalanche of debris.

Great walls began to emerge from the hill, gateways, sacrificial altars and ramps. Schliemann observed traces of a fire, he found the "well-paved street that led from the temple to the Palace of Priam," and he discovered the Scaean Gate where Achilles was killed by an arrow shot from Paris' bow.

To make sure that these slabs of stone were not removed secretly, Schliemann told the Christians among his workmen that Jesus of Nazareth had passed through this gate on a visit to King Priam and that the Savior had touched these stones with his own hands. The story made a great impression on the Turks. They would not remove a single stone that belonged to this gateway.

But everything else dug out of the hill was in constant danger of being looted by greedy peasants or disloyal workmen. When Schliemann went to Athens for a short time, even one of the overseers yielded to the temptation to enrich himself by dishonest means. He sold some of the well hewn stones and told Schliemann that they would be used to build a bell tower and houses. The man was dismissed. The new watchman was a giant of a man with a loaded musket. At least the bigger blocks which were not so easy to remove, were now safe from thieves.

It was May when Schliemann discovered the Scaean Gate, two and a half years after the dig had begun. One hundred thousand objects had been found and assembled, enough for Schliemann to fill a whole museum. He planned to publish a book of his discoveries with two hundred plates and three thousand five hundred steel engravings.

A fire destroyed the log cabin on the hill and Sophia only just escaped being burned to death. The land began to scorch in the increasing drought. There were scorpions wherever one walked. Vipers no thicker than a man's little finger slithered over the blocks and darted out of cracks in the earth.

41

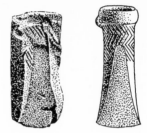

Drainpipe mold with reconstructed
drainpipe beside it. Troy

There was insubordination among the workmen and Schliemann began to grow nervous about them, as well as about the snakes and scorpions whose numbers increased in spite of all the countermeasures they took. Sometimes he rode into a nearby village to visit a Greek merchant, a man who had been born without feet. He spoke Italian and French and knew a large portion of the *Iliad* by heart. It was under this man's roof that Schliemann sought the companionship of a man who understood what his work meant.

In spite of all his finds, he had to fight his own doubts. Instead of the buildings Homer had described, he found walls, vessels, utensils and equipment from widely different periods. Only once did he find a skeleton adorned with jewelry, a gold hairpin and gold earrings. The abundance of ornaments that he discovered among his finds was puzzling. The swastika, which had been known as a symbol of the sun in all ancient civilizations, recurred so often that he planned to write a book about it.

From Berlin and Paris, from scholars throughout the world, there came hostile criticisms. Expressions of approval were much rarer, for only a few people appreciated the true extent of his work. Schliemann felt tired. During those two and a half years, there was only one person he could truly rely on and that was Sophia, his wife.

On May 30, Schliemann wrote to his son Sergei' in Moscow, telling him that his excavations at Troy were completed.

The Treasure of Priam

That same day, Schliemann wrote another letter, this time to Frederick Calvert, the brother of Frank. This is what it said: "I am sorry to inform you that I am closely watched and expect that the Turkish overseer, who is angry with me, I do not know for what reason, will search my house tomorrow. I, therefore, take the liberty to deposit with you six baskets and a bag, begging you will kindly lock them up and not allow by any means the Turks to touch them."

What had happened? What was in that knapsack and those six baskets which Schliemann sent off in such secrecy to the man who owned half the hill of Hissarlik?

In the early morning of that May 30, 1873 (or else not long before—Schliemann never disclosed the exact date) there were workmen digging all over the site. In this way, Schliemann made it impossible for Amin Effendi, the observer, to see everything as it was excavated. Schliemann, Sophia, and three workmen were digging at the outer fortification wall, not far from the Scaean Gate and Priam's palace. Twenty five or thirty feet down Schliemann came across "a large copper object of the most remarkable shape." It lay like a shield as if hiding something. Schliemann saw at once that concealed beneath it there was gold. In a flash, he covered up his discovery with earth and stones.

Then he called to Sophia and he gave her an order that she found very strange. She was to go and shout "Paidos! Paidos!" for everyone on the site to hear. "Paidos" is a word of uncertain derivation that means "time to stop work."

"What, now?" asked Sophia in astonishment. "At seven o'clock in the morning?"

"Do as I tell you," insisted Schliemann and added: "Tell the people that it's my birthday and they may all go home."

Then Sophia saw by Schliemann's face that he must have come

43

across something extraordinary. She climbed one of the rickety ladders to the top of the mound and called aloud "Paidos!" Everyone was surprised, but when she informed them all that it was Schliemann's birthday and he was giving his men the day off, there were cheers and everyone went home. Apparently Amin Effendi considered himself one of Schliemann's men too, for he too went off, without any misgivings, for it so happened that in the last few weeks hardly anything had been found that could have been carried off.

Sophia climbed down again to where Schliemann was standing and she told him that apart from themselves, there was no one left on the hill of Hissarlik. Then Schliemann cleared away the earth with which he had safeguarded his discovery.

Above the shield-like copper object, there lay a five foot thick layer of rubble and red ash, baked into a stone hard slab when Troy went up in flames. This bore the whole weight of the forti-

Page from Schliemann's diary, April 14, 1873

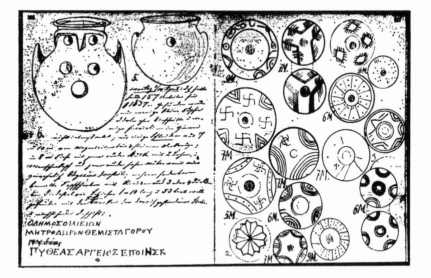

fication wall, built of rough stones and earth and twenty one feet in height. Schliemann, therefore, had to rely on that calcined crust for his safety, but the sight of the gold made him oblivious to every danger.

With his pocket knife, he cut the treasure out of the surrounding earth and piece by piece he laid it on his wife's red shawl: first of all, a copper shield and a helmet with a pair of horns; then a copper kettle and copper plates, silver dishes and silver cups, copper daggers, spear heads, and silver knives. And finally came the gold: drinking bowls, of which the largest weighed just under a pound and a half, diadems made of numerous gold chains, gold earrings, circlets and bracelets, innumerable gold rings, pierced dice and bead-like buttons, all of gold. There were eight thousand seven hundred and fifty gold rings alone when they counted them later. Schliemann also found a copper object that at first he believed must be the key to the treasure chest, but later it turned out to be a chisel.

Schliemann was sure that he had found the "Treasure of Priam." No one was watching as he carried it away to his wooden hut. There, with trembling hands, he placed on his wife's head a diadem made of ninety gold chains. A mesh of delicate gold rings covered the brow like a veil, and petals and leaves of gold hung down to her shoulders.

"Helen!" he exclaimed as Sophia stood before him wearing the jewels of Troy. Only once again in his life was Schliemann granted a moment of such magnitude—when he looked on the face of Agamemnon.

The problem now was how to stop the "Treasure of Priam" from being confiscated and here Schliemann emerged as a true Odysseus. Before Amin Effendi had time to suspect anything and have Schliemann's house searched, the treasure had gone. It was on its way in six baskets and a knapsack to an estate near Bunarbashi which belonged to Frederick Calvert, the consul's brother. A few days later, those baskets crossed the frontier.

Schliemann made the Turkish customs officers drunk, and told them that there was Trojan fruit in those baskets. His wife, he said, preferred it to all the fruit in Greece.

On June 17, the workmen were paid off abruptly. A priest blessed what was left of the Trojan hill. Schliemann arrived in Athens two days later with the most valuable part of the treasure.

In Athens, he promptly published his great discovery. He wrote letters all over the world and articles for the newspaper, the *Augsburger Allgemeine*. The gold of Troy he cited as proof that he was right when he maintained that Troy had actually existed and that the war described by Homer had really taken place. The world listened and Schliemann became famous over-night in Germany, in England, everywhere.

William Gladstone, the British Prime Minister, supported Schliemann and his views. Renowned explorers and scholars acknowledged his discovery as being one of the highest order. Others, though, were dubious, especially learned professors in Germany.

The most important development of all, however, was that the Turkish government now turned against Schliemann. They accused him of double-crossing them disgracefully, and demanded the return of the Trojan treasure.

Schliemann still practicing the cunning of an Odysseus, made the gold disappear forthwith. It was hidden away in barns and stables at the homes of Sophia's relatives. When Schliemann's house in Athens was searched, not one gold ring could be found.

Turkey forced Greece to prosecute Schliemann. The case dragged on for a whole year and in the end, he was sentenced to a fine of ten thousand francs. Schliemann voluntarily paid Turkey five times the amount of the fine, and he sent back a number of crates containing some of the articles he had found. But the treasure was now his own property, and he offered it to Greece, in exchange for permission to excavate Mycenae.

When this permit was refused, he wrote letters offering it to museums in London, Paris, St. Petersburg and Rome, but always

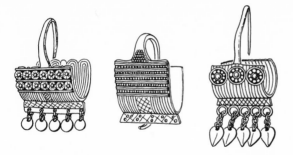

Golden earrings. Troy

on certain conditions, with a view to making the most of his discoveries. In the end, it was a great scientist and doctor named Virchow, the man who was Schliemann's most influential friend apart from Gladstone, who was able to assure the Trojan treasures for Berlin.

Schliemann was given the freedom of the German capital, a signal mark of distinction that he shared only with Bismarck and Moltke. And when the German Emperor too bestowed exceptional honors on Schliemann, he decided to donate the gold of Troy to "the nation he most loved and esteemed."

After an exhibition in London, the treasure was donated permanently to the Berlin Museum for Pre- and Ancient History.

A short report on its subsequent fate may be added here. When the bombing raids of the Second World War began, the gold from the Schliemann collection was deposited for safekeeping first in the vaults of the Prussian State Bank and then in an air-raid shelter in the Berlin Zoo. An intensive air attack buried both the bank and the shelter. Most of the rest of the Trojan collection was taken for safety to Castle Lebus on the east bank of the Elbe river. This castle was looted at the end of the war, and in the years that followed it was scheduled for demolition.

An archaeologist received permission to go to the villages around Castle Lebus to find out what had happened to the Trojan relics from the Schliemann collection. She took with her twenty five pounds of candy and approached the local children. And they brought her Trojan dishes and jugs that had managed to

47

find their way from the castle into the kitchen cupboards of the peasantry. Many of them were deliberately broken by the children to get extra sweets and later on the archaeologist found out that at country weddings, it was the custom to stamp on broken crocks and "other old junk" from the castle during the dancing. None of the wedding guests had any idea what they were trampling underfoot as they danced. Still some of the Trojan ceramics were saved, but there was no trace of the gold that Schliemann found in Hissarlik in May 1873.

Today, "Trojan Gold" can be seen only in the Istanbul Museum. It includes gold jewelry that two of Schliemann's workmen found and kept for themselves, without being caught at the time. Most of it had been hidden in a vase shaped like an owl's head. One of the men had gone straight to a goldsmith and had his share made into a thick gold necklace with a flower pattern. The other man hid his portion somewhere in his house. One day when he was out, his wife came across it accidentally. She put it on and went out to the market. She was arrested and interrogated, her husband was locked up and tortured and thus the theft came to light. In the gold collection of the Turkish Museum there are also gold and silver rings, gold bars and little golden balls, a circlet and some studs, which Schliemann discovered on his sixth dig at Troy on October 21, 1878, accompanied by officers frm a British warship. These articles were found close to the same fortification wall where Schliemann had made his first exciting finds.

The "Treasure of Priam", wrested from beneath the debris of a war of annihilation, probably lies buried once again under the rubble and the ruins. Or else it has been hidden away in some very remote hiding place. A much more important gold treasure, however, also found by Schliemann, has survived the Second World War and is on display at the National Museum in Athens. Three years after the Trojan finds, it was brought to light at the Palace of Mycenae, near the Lion Gate.

Opposite: (Above) Mycenae, shaft grave circle within the walls
(Below) The Lion Gate at Mycenae

The Great Discovery by the Lion Gate

When Schliemann first put spade to soil at Mycenae, a year after his return from his successful dig at Troy, he had no permit to do so. Secretly he hired a few workmen and had them sink thirty four test pits as quickly as possible. After five days, he was caught red-handed and charges were brought against him. The police descended on him and his assistants but Schliemann did not lose his head. He calmly invited the senior officer to have a cup of coffee and he showed him the fragments he had found, which were lying around in baskets. The officer, who should have started proceedings, instead reported to his superiors that Herr Schliemann had collected only worthless junk, "which any-one strolling around the ruins can pick up for himself." To be sure, Schliemann was told that he was "absolutely forbidden" to do any more digging and a permanent watch was placed to protect Mycenae from any further outrages. The authorities in Athens had every reason to take such precautions.

Meanwhile, the way in which Schliemann had walked off with the gold of Troy was a topic on everyone's lips. And if it so happened that the Greek court had sentenced him to pay a petty fine only and did not order him to return the treasure, that was largely because the plaintiffs in this case were Greece's arch-enemies, the Turks. Herr Schliemann must not be allowed to repeat the performance on Greek soil, not at any price.

There remained no alternative, then, but for him to sign a contract with the Archaeological Society of Greece, in which he undertook to hand over to them everything he found, and to accept the presence of three permanent observers or overseers.

As soon as the permission to excavate in Greece reached Schliemann, he began to do so, but not in Mycenae. In July 1876, he went to Tiryns, and inside the mighty castle walls which, according to legend, had been built by seven Cyclops from the plains of Troy, he had several test trenches dug. But in August he called it off. He announced his decision to defer no longer the "much more important excavation of Mycenae." He wanted to uncover the "Citadel" and the "Treasury", which were situated near the Lion Gate. What he said was this: "Now that Troy has been excavated, I know that I can render scholarship no greater service than to dig up Mycenae."

So he left Tiryns and crossed the plains that Homer calls "Argos where the horses graze," now burnt dry in the summer's heat. He traveled northward along the dusty roads, through sun-colored corn and tobacco fields, until he saw two naked peaks rearing their heads before him, with the fortress of Mycenae crouching between them. The nearer Schliemann approached, the more this hill grew into a mountain. Beneath the pale August sky, it loomed ahead like some huge, long forgotten helmet, beneath which a secret lies, concealed for all time.

The hill, which is eight hundred eighty-six feet high, has grown into a wilderness in the course of the last three thousand years. All that remains are the ruins of its Cyclopean walls and the two stone lions. A deep ravine protects the southern flank of the mountain. The cateract that has sawn its way through the living rock and down to the bottom of the precipice, is called Chaos. From the south the fortress is impregnable.

Schliemann, who had made his great discovery at Troy immediately below a wall and near a gateway, wished to start digging close to the Lion Gate at Mycenae, where the walls are up to sixteen feet thick.

Unlike the site of Troy, which had been violently disputed, it had been well known throughout the centuries where Agamemnon "King of Men" had had his palace. There were even references to the royal graves of Mycenae in old books and it was the excavation of these tombs that Schliemann had set his heart on. The key to the whole enterprise was contained in the works of the Greek author, Pausanias, who had written a kind of guide

Gateway to the 'Treasury of Atreus'. c. 36 ft. high. Reconstruction according to Marinatos. The delicacy of the decoration cannot possibly be reproduced on the much reduced scale of this drawing.

book to Ancient Greece about 175 A.D. This is what it had to say about Agamemnon's citadel. "Parts of the wall are still preserved, as well as the gate over which the lions stand. These also they say are the work of the Cyclops who built the wall for Proteus at Tiryns. In the ruins of Mycenae there is a fountain called Perseia and underground buildings of Atreus and his sons where their treasures were. There is the tomb of Atreus . . . the tomb of Agamemnon . . . of Eurymedon the charioteer, and that of the twins . . . to whom Cassandra gave birth . . . and one of Electra. Clytemnestra and Aegisthus were buried a little outside the wall, for they were not deemed worthy of burial within it, where Agamemnon lies and those who were murdered with him."

Agamemnon, Cassandra and Electra were real people not mythical figures for Pausanias, the ancient travel guide, just as they were for Schliemann. Pausanias, too, had a thorough knowledge of the events of the Trojan War; he also knew Homer by heart. That made him a reliable authority as far as Schliemann was concerned.

Now Schliemann interpreted many of the things that he read in Pausanias differently from the classical scholars, especially the description of the location of the graves. The scholars believed that Pausanias meant the outer walls of the town itself, which had also included the lower part of the city. They thought that the royal graves must lie far away from the Lion Gate. Schliemann, on the contrary, told himself that Pausanias had lived a good fourteen hundred years after Agamemnon's return from Troy, that is, at a time when the whole of the lower city as well as the outer walls that once enclosed it, had completely vanished from the earth's surface. What Schliemann saw when he visited Mycenae was the same scene that greeted the eyes of Pausanias too. By 'wall', he could only have meant the one which contains the Lion Gate. And it was at that spot, watched over by the two stone lions, that Schliemann wanted to try his luck.

On August 7, the hottest day of the year, he began his task.

On August 19, he announced that he and his one hundred and twenty five workmen were making good progress. The three overseers, though, under a man called Stamatakis, proved a great nuisance. There were clashes between Schliemann and Stamatakis almost every day.

The latter had been given strict instructions. The remains of the walls must be left standing. Anything that seemed precarious must be shored up as Schliemann went along, and before he dug any farther.

Schliemann distributed his workers over a wide field. He spurred on their enthusiasm, rewarding even the smallest find, so that it was impossible for the observers to keep an eye on everything. Stamatakis wrote exasperated letters to Athens. "This man ruthlessly destroys anything that seems unimportant to him. He keeps me dashing about the whole day in the scorching heat, and then I have to sit with him until two o'clock in the morning examining all his finds. I am utterly exhausted."

But Schliemann had no pity on Stamatakis, and said he was forever finding fault. He called those who got in his way, "idiots who haven't the least idea of what is at stake here." This time he had no intention of running off with what he found, but he would not be interfered with by anyone, neither by local officials nor by ministers' envoys. He stalked around with blazing eyes and as soon as Stamatakis dared to utter a single word, Schliemann would pounce on him like a wild animal that had better not be provoked. Sophia was always stepping in to try and keep the peace.

Schliemann had men digging in three places simultaneously; at the Lion Gate; in the ground nearby; and at the Treasury of Atreus. Here and at the Lion Gate, he found that the earth was as hard as stone. He uncovered a porter's lodge by the Lion Gate, a low, and rather forbidding cell, whose ceiling consisted of one single slab of stone. Schliemann found no sign of the slightest comfort here, but as he asserts, "In the heroic ages,

Battle scene from funerary stele. Mycenae

luxury was quite unknown to the common people and so it was not missed."

He had better luck at the pits inside the palace wall, for there he came upon the remains of a water duct and two beautiful stone reliefs, one of which showed a charioteer going into battle, and the other a hunting scene. Schliemann took them as promising omens.

But no further finds of outstanding value turned up in the next few weeks. There were indeed painted potsherds, earthenware figures and clay animals: millstones, axes and knives; fragments of rock crystal, arrowheads, combs, boars' teeth and ivory pins, and last of all, a golden stud. Schliemann had the men dig deeper still wherever finds were made. Soon he came across a circle of man-high stone slabs or steles, which stood in two rows three feet apart and had once been roofed to make a covered perimeter.

Schliemann believed that this ring was the *agora* or place of assembly for the people of Mycenae. It was so important a place that he guessed immediately he would find the grave of Agamemnon here. For the *agora* was considered holy ground, the center of the town, the place where decisions were made concerning peace and war, where the gods were invoked and where heroes and artists were honored.

It remains a puzzle to know why Schliemann did not go on excavating here right away. Instead, he uncovered a big building south of this circle, one which lay much lower down the hillside. Schliemann believed that he had stumbled on the palace of Agamemnon, but apart from axes, weapons and stone whorls, nothing more exciting was discovered until a big vessel was brought to light, a capacious vase. On it was painted a procession of warriors in red, and Schliemann was fascinated when he saw it.

These warriors are wearing helmets, cuirasses and greaves. In the left hand, they carry a round shield and in the right a spear, with a bottle dangling from it. The helmets have a metal horn

Procession of warriors, from the 'Warrior Vase'. Mycenae

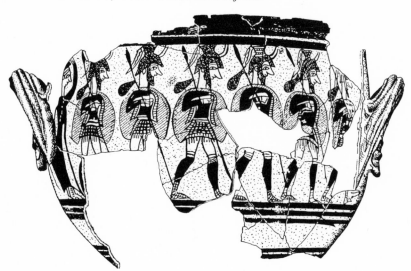

or a boar's tusk fitted, and they are trimmed with tufts of feathers and horns.

Schliemann saw that it portrayed a troop of Trojan warriors. In one passage in the *Iliad*, these horned helmets are mentioned. It reads: "Menelaus drew his silver mounted sword and swung it down on the horn of the enemy's helmet. But the sword broke and fell from his hand."

Nothing made Schliemann happier than to find even this detail in Homer confirmed by his finds.

Two blazing months went by among the bare hills. The workmen were exhausted from digging into the stone hard earth. This endless digging wore down even Schliemann as well as Sophia who spared herself as little as her husband. In the middle of October, the rains began to fall. Near the Treasury, which was not far from the Lion Gate, Sophia was in charge of one working party. A wall of limestone blocks prevented further progress and had to be removed. When at last, after laborious efforts, the diggers succeeded in entering the domed chamber, they found a gold leaf on the threshold.

From November onward, instead of the scorching heat, they had rain and mud to contend with. For weeks on end, it looked as if they would discover nothing of serious significance at Mycenae.

Then, on December 6, when Schliemann was having another closer look at the place where he had discovered the stone reliefs with the hunting scene and the war chariot, he chanced upon the first grave. He found long, hewn slabs, ashes, ornaments carved from bone and little golden disks.

A cloudburst turned the grave into a morass, so Schliemann moved on to the nearby gravestone and had it lifted. A second grave emerged, which yielded three skeletons at a depth of nearly fifteen feet. Sophia cleaned the mud from them with the utmost care. Near each skeleton were found five gold diadems, fourteen gold crosses, a silver goblet and fragments of vases.

56

The three corpses had been buried with their heads towards the east.

In a third grave, three more skeletons were discovered. They were adorned much more lavishly, with gold crowns whose upper edge was fringed with gold leaves, eight in all; in addition, there were six gold jugs, necklaces, jugs with gold lids and seven hundred little gold plates, decorated in shapes of stars, flowers, cuttle fish and butterflies. In addition, there were bronze daggers with double-edged blades and a wealth of gold jewelry.

Above the northern wall of the third tomb, exactly in the center of the stone circle there hung a menacing block of stone, which Schliemann thought must have been a speaker's tribune. With alarm he noticed that the block was split. The deeper they burrowed, the greater was the danger for the workmen and for Schliemann himself. The men were growing reckless after the rapidly increasing number of finds and they dug away as enthusiastically as if there were nothing but the empty sky above them. As in Troy, Schliemann was only just in time to pull aside the workmen when the block worked itself loose and was shattered to fragments as it fell with a terrible crash. Schliemann and two of his assistants were hurt by flying splinters of stone.

In Pausanias, five graves were mentioned. Schliemann had now uncovered three of them. Encouraged by this success, he began clearing the ground right next to the tomb they had discovered last, although the spot was not marked by a slab. The discoloration of the earth around aroused Schliemann's suspicions, for one spot was darker than the surrounding soil.

When the men had dug to a depth of sixteen feet, they found some earthenware sherds. About three feet deeper still, there was a wall, which at first looked like the coping of a well. It was an altar. Schliemann took its measurements, made a drawing of it, then had it broken up and went on digging.

At last, twenty six feet down, they found the skeletons of five people. As in other graves, they were bedded on a layer of flints, three with their heads to the east and two to the north. The five corpses were laden with gold and jewels. Three of them wore gold masks. Near one of the corpses, lay a crushed gold object which at first Schliemann took to be a helmet. On closer examination, it turned out to be a lion's head. Besides these, there were found in the grave two golden cuirasses, a tall gold crown with leaves that were fastened so loosely to the crown itself that they fluttered with the slightest movement. There were eleven beakers of massive gold, gold girdles, buckles and brooches, more than five hundred gold plates, four hundred pieces of gold and double axes of gold; ten gold dishes, a bull's head with gold horns and a gold cuttlefish.

The most precious of all for Schliemann was a gold cup with handles on which two doves were perched. Homer had given a precise description of a similar cup in the *Iliad:* "It was decorated with studs and with two doves facing each other, feeding." This was the golden goblet of Nestor, the gray-haired King of Pylos.

The fifth grave Schliemann discovered a few paces northwest of the fourth one. In contrast to the graves they had found so far, it was not lined with stone and there was only one body in it. Around the head there was a broad gold diadem and at its left side, there was a gold cup but this grave seemed poor in comparison to the wealth in the other tombs.

Now Schliemann went back to the first grave. The weather had remained fine and the mud had dried out. With the greatest

Embossed golden discs, diameter approx. 2½". Mycenae

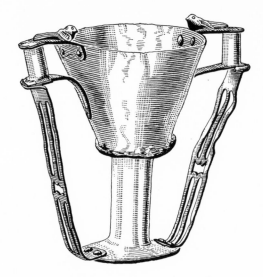

Golden 'Cup of Nestor'.
Mycenae

care, he dug right down to the bottom. There he found three bodies, the middle one of which had hardly any ornaments. Obviously a grave robber had sunk a narrow shaft, come upon this corpse, and stolen most of the valuable objects, the golden mask, armor and weapons. As he fled in haste, small objects like gold buttons and disks had dropped back into the grave, or else the robber was so afraid of being discovered that he did not bother to pick everything up.

The other two corpses, however, were stiff with gold. There were eighty wafer-thin rapiers with gold hilts, and gold cups too had been placed by their side. There were masks of gold and gold breastplates. One of the two masks was much finer than any discovered so far. This golden countenance stared at Schliemann, stern yet composed. The eyes looked as if they were open, although the lids were shut. Schliemann was so moved that he raised the mask to his lips and kissed it. Then, thunderstruck, he saw that the face which the mask had covered was actually intact. Schliemann had looked a King of Mycenae in the face.

59

Golden 'Mask of Agamemnon'.
Mycenae

He had not the slightest doubt that it was Agamemnon, whom he had intended to find from the start.

Now he had succeeded and at the eleventh hour too, as had happened so miraculously at Troy. Schliemann was deeply concerned that the head might disintegrate. He telegraphed for help and had the corpse embalmed. An artist painted a picture of the head in order to preserve it. Then with the utmost care, the stone slab on which the corpse was laid, was chiseled out of the living rock and sawn free.

Schliemann sent the following telegram to the King of Greece: "With extreme joy I announce to Your Majesty that I have discovered the tombs which tradition has designated as the sepulchres of Agamemnon, Cassandra, Eurymedon and all their companions who were killed while partaking of a meal with Clytemnestra and her lover Aegisthus . . . I believe I have gazed on the face of Agamemnon."

Agamemnon's Avenger

The news of the discovery of the royal graves ran around the world like wildfire. The scholars sat up and took notice. Thousands flocked to Mycenae to see the graves from which Schliemann had extracted treasure far exceeding in value his earlier finds at Troy. They came to see Agamemnon, and also this strange man who had used his personal riches to look for the gold of Troy and Mycenae.

Schliemann had grown into a legend himself, the penniless boy who had become a millionaire, and whose good fortune in the archaeological field was quite unparalleled.

In Mycenae, on a hill big enough to house a whole city, he had confined his digging to an area about one hundred thirty feet square, and it was in this small plot that he had found the five tombs mentioned by Pausanias. And not only gold crowns, goblets and swords had been found in the graves, but seventeen corpses as well, of whom five were godlike kings with faces of gold. For Schliemann, it was final proof of his firm conviction that the events in the *Iliad* and the *Odyssey* had actually happened.

Agamemnon had really lived. After the fall of Troy, Hephaistos had indeed kindled the pyre of victory on Mount Ida and on the Isle of Lemnos, on Mount Athos and on the Messager Mountains. And on all the heights where posts had been manned for ten long years, flaming beacons passed the signal from island to island, and peak after peak blazed with the tidings: Troy has fallen, the war is over, the heroes are coming home! Near the look-out tower above Mycenae, the last column of flame had leapt into the air and Aegisthus and Clytemnestra had stared into the sky above them, and they had seen that it was as red as blood. Night after night, Schliemann too had lit a watch fire once the graves had been found. No mischief maker should enter the circle that was marked by a double row of man-high slabs.

For weeks Schliemann guarded his finds until everything had been taken to safety in Athens, crowns and jewels, masks, daggers and cups, and all the other precious articles. He kept scrupulously to the agreement that he had made with the Greeks a year before. Without hesitation, he handed over all the different objects he had extracted from the graves of Mycenae.

He had enough left, after all, things that no one could wrest from him. After immense sacrifices and hardships he had achieved the success he had dreamed of since he was ten, to see Troy and Agamemnon with his own eyes.

That night, before he returned to Athens, he kept vigil by the fire that burned continuously above the circle of graves. He had sent away all his helpers even Sophia, who had shared with him the tremendous task at Mycenae. Now she was asleep and he wanted to be alone with those whom his excavations had resurrected.

For a long time he sat gazing into the glowing embers, crimson and purple like the carpets that Clytemnestra had spread along the path leading from the Lion Gate to the King's Hall.

Palace of Mycenae, reconstruction of the northwest corner, according to Wace

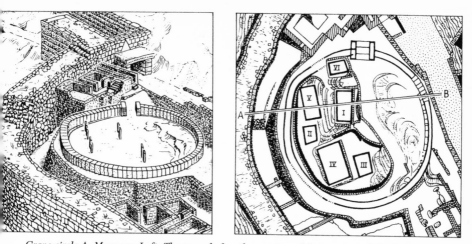

Grave circle A, Mycenae. Left: The agora before the opening of the graves, with back view of the Lion Gate beyond. Right: Bird's eye view of the six open graves.

Agamemnon, the victor of Troy, had stepped across them un-suspecting and the people of Mycenae had cheered their Prince to the echo. The heroes had come home at last and they caroused and feasted until far into the night, toasted by those who had stayed behind. Palace and town had been kept awake all night by the noise of unrestrained reveling. At dawn, how-ever, when most of the merrymakers lay on the ground, stupe-fied and drunk, the cries of men in the throes of death had shaken the mighty walls and Agamemnon's own palace had be-come a trap, where he and his followers together with Cassandra and her two children, had been slaughtered like cattle.

In the glow, Schliemann saw Agamemnon's countenance, the golden mask that a god has for his face. It seemed incredible that a ruler of such stature should have been slain so treacher-ously by the woman who had borne him three children.

Schliemann raised his eyes and saw himself surrounded by shadows. Much evil had been wrought inside these walls, within the Lion Gate. From the very first, gods and men had prepared

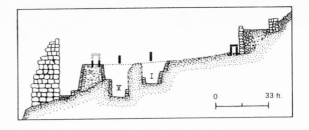

Section through the grave circle, corresponding to the line A–B in illustration on preceding page. The positions of the stelae above the graves shown in right illustration, preceding page are marked I and V.

the ground for violence and treachery. In a dark chain of gruesome events, the dynasty founded by Atreus was laid low. Brother had betrayed brother, women their menfolk and kings their children. The sun had stopped in its course, aghast, when Atreus, who was Agamemnon's father, had offered Thyestes, his own brother, the flesh of his children to eat at table. With a curse on his lips, Thyestes had fled and it was his son Aegisthus, who had avenged the grisly deed on Agamemnon, son of Atreus, when he and Clytemnestra slew the king on his return home from Troy.

Another shadow stepped out of the darkness toward the fire.

"Who are you?"

"I am Orestes."

"You killed Aegisthus."

"Yes, and my mother too."

"You did but obey the oracle."

The shade lingered. As if he were standing trial once more, Orestes defended himself. "I was a mere child when my father offered his daughter Iphigenia as a sacrifice, so that he should have fair winds when he set off for the war. When he had left, Electra, my other sister, sent me away from home secretly, because she feared that Aegisthus might kill me. I grew up abroad,

64

Opposite: Mycenaean frescoes. (Above) Cretan-mycenaean demons (Below) Ladies on a grandstand

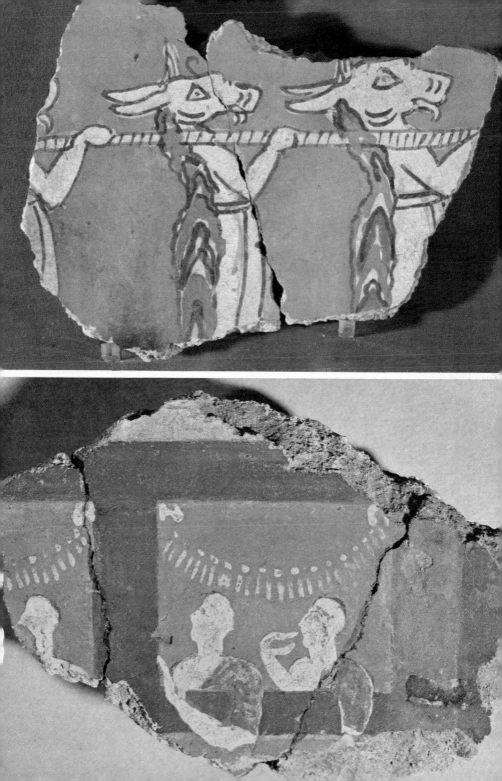

and Pylades, the son of a king who had not joined in the Trojan expedition, became my friend. After my mother had murdered my father, I returned to Mycenae as a stranger and not even Electra recognized me as her brother when we met at the spot where they had buried Agamemnon, Prince of Men. It was Electra who gave me the sword with which I was to kill my mother, and this I did, for it is an Achaean's first duty above all others to avenge his father's death.

"After this, I was made King of Mycenae, and yet the Furies pounced on me and hounded me from place to place, so that the world became a living hell. I had killed my mother, it is true, but I had only done what Apollo, the god, had bade me do at his oracle. Half crazed as I was, I returned to Delphi to consult the oracle once more. Then the voice of the god spoke: Go hence to Colchis, it said, and bring a sister back with you. Then you will have expiated your crime.

"I knew that in a temple at Colchis there was a likeness of Artemis, the sister of Apollo and this is what I thought I must fetch. Pylades went with me and then the miracle happened. I found Iphigenia whom I had believed dead. She had been spirited away from the sacrificial altar and taken to Colchis by Artemis. So instead of the god's sister, I brought my own sister home. That was Apollo's wish for he kept his word and spoke on my behalf before the tribunal. The Furies had to let me go, the curse was lifted from the House of Atreus, and I, the last King of Mycenae, was the first who was allowed to reign here in peace."

The ghost fell silent. Schliemann started from his dream and saw that the fire had burned low. He began to feel the icy cold. He could see clearly the dark openings to the five graves from which he had extracted so many remarkable things, treasure that had lain hidden there for more than three thousand years. He got to his feet and walked away, through the Lion Gate. It was time to leave for Athens. His work at Mycenae was done.

Opposite: Cyclopean sally port, citadel of Mycenae

The World of the Achaeans

In Athens, Schliemann wrote a book about his excavations at Mycenae, filling more than two hundred pages with the descriptions of what he had found. The book was also a tribute to Sophia. For twenty five days, she had worked on her knees, scraping the earth so carefully from wafer-thin swords and crowns, precious vessels and other articles, that not a thing was damaged in the process. More even than at Troy, she had shown herself to be her husband's equal and helpmate, who not only dug tirelessly all day, but several times prevented the excavation from ending in disaster by her sensible intervention. Once, for instance, she took it upon herself to burn a letter of Schliemann's in the flame of a candle. He had intended her to hand it to the Greek Minister of Education, but it would have caused serious offense in high places. She destroyed the letter and by her tactful words, she was able to convince the Minister in person that no one but Schliemann could bring the great undertaking at Mycenae to a successful conclusion.

Schliemann never went back to Mycenae as an excavator. He had discovered five graves there and as Pausanias had only mentioned five, Schliemann simply took it for granted that there were no more tombs to be found there. He had also uncovered everything else mentioned by Pausanias besides the graves, the Treasury of Atreus and the Lion Gate with its humble janitor's lodge. He had descended to the spring of Perseia which had supplied the citadel and the acropolis with water; he had also admired the subterranean passage through which it was possible to fetch this water in times of siege, beneath the feet of the enemy. Accurate measurements had been taken of the King's Hall in which Agamemnon had met his death and of the remains of walls and staircases. Schliemann wrote his book, convinced that nothing of importance has escaped him.

One January day, he sent his assistant Drosinos to Mycenae, to make a careful plan of the grave circle. As he sketched, Drosinos noticed that there were several roughly hewn stones that seemed identical with the horizontal slabs which Schliemann had found. He mentioned his observations to Stamatakis who had watched Schliemann with such mistrust during the excavations and had now been left in charge at Mycenae.

A workman was called. With Stamatakis and Drosinos watching, the man began to dig. Soon a golden goblet came to light and half an hour later, there were four of them. Gold jewelry and signet rings of great beauty were found, but no bodies.

One of the signet rings is particularly remarkable. On it is depicted a goddess sitting under a tree while priestesses bring her flowers. In the air hovers a child with a sword and a figure eight shield and a number of mysterious signs. Sun and moon are in the sky, it is noon and night simultaneously.

When Schliemann saw this seal, he thought at once of the passage in the *Iliad* where Homer describes the shield that Hephaistos made for Achilles, a shield of five layers on the uppermost part of which were shown "the earth, the sky, the sea, the tireless sun and the moon and the stars." Schliemann was convinced that Homer must have seen this strange seal which his adversary, Stamatakis, had obtained from the sixth Mycenean grave.

This was not the last grave to be discovered in Mycenae. Seventy five years after Schliemann's great finds, the Greek archaeologist Papadimitriu uncovered a second circle of slabs with shaft graves—six hundred fifty feet southwest of the Lion Gate, that is, outside the wall.

In these graves too lay Mycenean princes and princesses furnished with an amazing wealth of jewelry and weapons. Before that both a Greek named Tsountas, and Wace, an Englishman had dug in Mycenae with considerable success. They were both professional archaeologists who continued Schliemann's work, and learning from the experience of excavators elsewhere, they could correct many understandable errors.

Thus Schliemann had believed that the dead in these royal graves had been bedded on a funeral pyre, simply because Homer says that the bodies of the slain Achaeans were burned before Troy, Tsountas proved that no fire had ever been lit in any Mycenean grave. Schliemann had found slabs of slate in the graves,

Golden signet ring.
Height of seal $^9/_{10}$". Mycenae

and he had thought that originally they must have lined the walls of the shafts. There were "chests of sheet copper" too, which he imagined had served as headrests for the dead. Dörpfeld, a young architect, who was recognized as a leading archaeologist during the excavation of Olympia, realized after a more detailed investigation that these 'copper chests' had once contained wood and had been left open at one side. In fact, copper had been wrapped around to protect the ends of the beams, and the beams themselves had been put in place to carry slabs of slate, to roof over the bodies. In other words, the shaft graves had been vaults which could be reopened when need be for the burial of subsequent corpses. It was only much later that the shafts had been filled in and circled by the double ring of steles.

68

After the destruction of the town, they had been exposed to thirty centuries of wind and rain, and thus they had disappeared from sight beneath a layer of gravel and earth. It was this deposit that had preserved the graves from looters.

Schliemann tried to repeat his "excavator's luck" in another two Mycenean centers after his great triumph in Mycenae itself; in Orchomenos and in Tiryns.

Orchomenos, like Mycenae was referred to by Homer as "the golden realm". Schliemann, however, found no gold in Orchomenos. He discovered a Treasury which, like those of Mycenae, lay below ground level and was domed like a beehive. Schliemann knew by now that these subterranean stone beehives which were approached through deep cut passages with mighty walls, were not hiding places or safe deposits but fortresses for the dead. The beehive tomb of Orchomenos had been broken into

Plan of the Citadel of Tiryns, about 12 miles south of Mycenae. In black: The palace proper—acropolis. Dotted: Inner citadel with west bastion and portico. Shaded: Lower citadel and casemates. 1 Ramp; 2 Main outer gateway, east; 3 Three other gateways, partly of wood; 4 Forecourt; 5 Outer forecourt; 6 Outer palace yard; 7 Inner courts; 8 Megaron (king's hall); 9 Inner citadel; 10 South and east casemates; 11 Tower of west bastion; 12 West gate; 13, 14, and 15 West, north, and east gates of lower citadel.

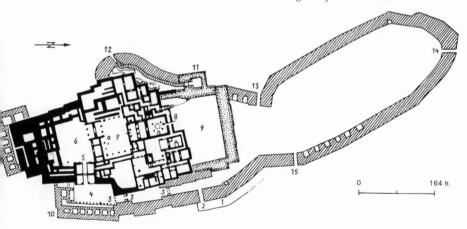

and was partly destroyed and, like the domed graves of Mycenae, it had already been looted. Of the citadel and town of Orchomenos, they found hardly any remains. All the more productive by comparison were the digs in Tiryns that Schliemann carried out together with Dörpfeld in 1884 and 1885.

One example will serve to show how objectively and boldly Dörpfeld went to work, as opposed to Schliemann who had read in Homer about palaces and temples and so in Troy and in Mycenean cities, he looked for temples. And when he found in Tiryns a room whose floor consisted of a huge stone slab, he believed he had found a shrine that had housed an altar.

Dörpfeld examined it more closely. There were some indications that the big limestone slab had formed the base of a cistern or water storage tank. Then he discovered that at the edges of the slab there were dowel holes for lengths of wood and by their arrangement, a trained architect could tell that there must have been a door at one side. Now no one would put a door in a tank or cistern, and a further discovery soon solved the riddle. Dörpfeld found ducts and a waste pipe. Now everything was clear. This was not a chapel but a bathroom. They did not have to wait long for final confirmation. Further excavations brought the actual remains of a bathtub to light. It was made of baked clay and decorated inside with paintings. The bathroom belonged to the prince's living quarters which were built next to the King's hall.

Later two German archaeologists, Karo and Müller, dug in Tiryns with considerable success. The whole of Greece was scoured for the ruins of Mycenean fortresses. In the rock chambers and a beehive grave at the citadel of Dendra Midea, a Swedish archaeological expedition found many wonderful gold ornaments, utensils, an ostrich egg mounted in gold and silver, and an iron ring which was evidently considered more valuable than many gold rings. At that time, iron was unknown in the whole of Greece, so the ring must have traveled a long way to get there, like the small disk of iron that Howard Carter found amid countless gold objects on the breast of the eighteen year old Pharaoh, Tutankhamen.

The archaeologists did not rest until they found the royal palace of the gray-haired Nestor on "sandy Pylos." It was not built on a rock as at Mycenae or Tiryns, but on a gentle and fertile ridge, overlooking a bay where ships are sheltered from the winds.

An American expedition under the leadership of Carl W. Blegen, has dug up the remains of Nestor's palace with such masterful skill that it is not difficult for the spectator to take in the site as a whole, to fill in the gaps in his imagination and to people the scene with figures. The Americans had fantastic luck in their digging. Their very first shaft struck the palace archives. Two rooms to which no looter had ever penetrated contained hundreds of small inscribed tablets of clay. In other rooms they came upon great heaps of unused pottery.

In all the Mycenean palaces weapons of war were the main finds. There were shields, spear tips, daggers and swords, mounted in gold and forged with exceptional care, as if these weapons were the key to life and not to death. Schliemann and those who followed in his footsteps had, by their discoveries, unlocked the entrance to a world of warriors.

As many as twelve swords each were laid in the graves of several of the Achaean princes. Five were a matter of course. In addition there were axes, javelins, helmets and turret-like shields as tall as a man. Hooks were placed inside these shields so that the owner could hang up his swords and other weapons. Thus these shields served as mobile cupboards or armories, as well as giving protection to the wearer. As the soldiers who took them into battle also wore body armor and greaves, they must certainly have been men of powerful strength to carry such a weight.

The Achaeans were infatuated with the art of war, which

brought them plunder and glory. This is revealed by their swords and daggers. They sparkle with agates and rock crystal, ivory, glass and faience. On the blades there may be battles with lions marvelously inlaid in gold and silver. On one hilt there are four lions' heads, but they are so arranged that they look like a flower with four petals. One has to look very closely indeed to make out their real faces. Lion helmets are not uncommon in Mycenean graves, and lions greet the visitor at the entrance to the palace gates of Mycenae, lions rampant to emphasize their power and grandeur.

The men who built the first citadels in Greece at a time when there were still lions to be hunted there, were lion-hearted too. They used for their fortresses blocks of masonry that only giants could shift. Many of these blocks are over ten feet long. The walls are so stout, they may be as much as fifty five feet thick and in places they tower to a height of thirty three feet. The walls of the sanctuary citadel of Gla are almost nine thousand eight hundred fifty feet long.

With the exception of Nestor's palace, these castles were all built on dominating heights. They frown menacingly down like warriors' aeries. The builders made good use of every advantage that Nature offered. The fortress of Mycenae is concealed in a natural ambush, a corner of "Argos where the horses graze," itself hidden but with a commanding view over the plains and dominating a network of roads. The Lion Gate was placed so that it was protected on three sides against attack. In addition there were two sally ports concealed in the wall. One of them guarded the hidden access to the spring.

Every Achaean citadel had its secret water supply. In the Acropolis at Athens even today, a concealed staircase descends in bold spirals through a crevice in the rock down to a subterranean spring. The Achaeans knew how to divert brooks and rivers into canals, to irrigate dry stretches of land and to turn marshes into good ploughland and pasture.

72

Centuries later, when the buildings themselves had long fallen into ruin their castles were still held in reverence by the Greeks. The people of Athens refused Pericles permission to pull down the "Pelasgian Wall," and so, because of the remains of the Mycenean castle, the building of the Propylaea was never completed at the southern corner. The memory of Achaean might and greatness was still too vivid. Under these bold princes and soldiers, fleets of ships set out from Greek harbors for the first time, making for distant coasts and deciding wars. They measured themselves against the very gods in combat, and Agamemnon, Prince of Men, held in his hands a scepter that came from Zeus himself.

Today we know more about the Achaeans than did the Greeks at the time of Pericles. Schliemann's discoveries alone would be sufficient for us to re-create a picture of their lives. In Tiryns, the fortress with the most powerful Cyclopean walls on Greek soil, Schliemann and Dörpfeld found countless fragments of frescoes which had once adorned the walls of the palace cham-

Wild boar hunt. Fresco
c. 17 ft. long. Tiryns

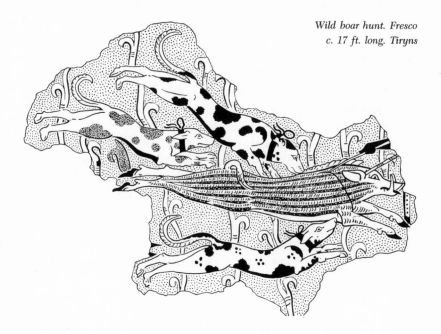

bers. Pieced together, these fragments show scenes with men and women, horses and chariots, dogs and game.

Danger is afoot; panthers, lions and wounded boars are hunted by women as well as men. Hunting dogs strain at the leash, red sandals glow, a wild boar is trapped in a net and pierced by spears. A piebald and a white horse fly side by side drawing a two-wheeled chariot driven by a woman. Horses are broken in, a castle is stormed. Wounded men tumble from the walls. From thousands of details which the archaeologists have brought to light one can reconstruct the daily life of the Achaeans. From the outside, their houses looked uninviting. Indoors, they used carpets, hangings, beautiful furniture, precious sofas made of plaited leather strips which had been brought home from military campaigns and foreign voyages. Their clothes too can be seen, for the women of Ithaca and Mycenae were skillful at weaving. In summer they wore short capes of lightweight materials, in winter long cloaks and fur gloves.

Their principal food was meat; mutton, goatsflesh and pork, as well as beef, game and poultry. Fish was not too popular but they appreciated oysters. Wine was sweetened with honey from the bees. In their orchards, they cultivated apples, pears, olives and figs. In the fields they grew lentils, beans and peas, millet, barley and corn. There were no domestic cats but they made up for them with dogs on every holding. When the men were not at sea or at war, they occupied their days with agriculture and hunting.

Even a prince knew how to hoist a sail and plough the land, as Odysseus says of himself not without a certain pride: "I only wish, Eurymachus, that you and I could compete as laborers in the early summer when the days draw out, in a hayfield somewhere, I with a crooked reaping-hook and you with its fellow, so that we could test each other at work, with nothing to eat till well after dusk and plenty of grass to cut. Or . . . I should choose a two-acre field with a clod that yielded nicely to the share. You'd see then whether I could cut a furrow straight ahead!"

In the Mycenean social order, everyone had his place. Kings, peasants, sailors and swineherds, potters and smiths, musicians and beggars. But the slave could become his master's trusted friend and every freeman could set out by ship to make his fortune if he were lucky, although he had to be prepared to surrender his liberty if he met with pirates and got the worst of the encounter.

Eumaios, the faithful swineherd of Odysseus, had been born a prince, the son of a king of Syria. This king had a young Phoenician slave girl and when a Phoenician ship from Sidon put to in Syria, a sailor persuaded the girl who understood his language, to run away with him. The girl agreed at the same time to kidnap the king's young son. While the ship was being loaded with cattle, hides, metals and wine, the sailor diverted the queen's attention by showing her an amber necklace. Eumaios was sold to Laertes and brought up in Ithaca where it was his task to look after the swine.

Throughout the Aegean Sea and all around their coasts, the Achaeans accomplished deeds which brought them fame and wealth. It was mainly Egyptian gold that was used for Mycenean death masks, breastplates, goblets and sword hilts. At that time, the Pharaohs had an empire to defend and so they were glad to take into their service soldiers of the same mettle as an Achilles. Gold from the Nile paid the wages of the Achaeans. From Egypt they imported their war chariots which had been introduced there by the Hyksos, a warlike people from Asia. And just as the Pharaohs were laid to rest in pyramids and in rock graves to rule in eternal palaces, so the Achaeans buried their dead in beehive graves, deep in the earth. They too wanted them to go on living after death, in the way they were accustomed to in the palaces that circled the peaks throughout the land like coronets of stone.

Through his excavations, Schliemann got to know the Achaeans better than anyone else, but even for him, the pioneer,
much remained a riddle. Meanwhile, eight decades have passed.
Eminent archaeologists have gone on working in the territory
where Schliemann first blazed the trail. And so today, a firm
answer can be given to many questions, even to the one: Where
did these princes and warriors come from who built Mycenae,
Tiryns, Orchomenos and Pylos, and who one day set out to
conquer Troy?

The Men who sacked Troy

From the days of Homer to those of Alexander who marched to India, the Greeks considered that their Achaean ancestors were "the first Greeks." It was impossible for them to imagine that any other people had ever lived on Greek soil. Since time immemorial, so they believed, Greek had been spoken in Greece even by the gods from whom the kings and heroes of the Achaeans were descended, which explained how gods and heroes could converse together and take part in the same battles and adventures. Zeus and Athene, Hera and Artemis, Apollo and Poseidon, it was taken for granted belonged to the Greek world as much as Herakles and Odysseus. For the Ancient Greeks, that was as solid a fact as Mount Olympus.

Then came the archaeologists and the philologists of our times, and they not only excavated buried cities and sunken graves, but they probed into everything that could throw a light upon the darkness of prehistoric days. They were only satisfied when they got down to the roots of things.

And then it transpired that the names of some of the Greek gods themselves, for instance, Athene, Hera and Artemis, were not Greek at all. Athens, Corinth and many other place names in Greece were not Greek either, nor were numerous words for plants, animals, and utensils.

Kastanon (chestnut), *kerasos* (cherry), *kyparissos* (cypress), *kithara* (zither), and numbers of other words which have passed from the Greek into many European languages, were introduced into Greek from foreign sources. Even that 'most Greek of all words' *"thalassa"*, the word for the sea, had a barbarian origin, that is, it was first used by non-Greeks, who brought it with them to Greece.

But where did all these foreign words come from?

The philologists followed the trail and it led them across the

Greek islands to the coast of Asia Minor where Troy lies. All along the way, the scholars came across places whose names, like Corinth or Kyparissos, ended in -inth or -issos. It was evident that hordes of migrants from Asia Minor had founded villages and even flourishing provinces on the isles and the Greek mainland. As the finds show, these people included highly skilled

Map of Greece and Asia Minor

craftsmen, who owned things of beauty, precious jewelry, pretty clothes, furniture and houses, who cultivated orchards and fields. They also traded goods, for the sea did not frighten them since they arrived on well-built ships. In short, they were people who had already achieved an astonishingly high level of civilization.

Long before there were Greek-speaking people in Greece, these tribes from the east had made their home in the Peloponnese, in Attica and Arcadia, as we know today for certain. In Tiryns and many other Greek palaces, the remains of round, Cyclopean buildings that were discovered date from the earliest times, and are much older than the Mycenean citadels. They are replicas of those to be found in Asia Minor.

These early migrants from the east settled throughout Greece and many regions at that time were more thickly populated than they are today. In Thessaly alone there were discovered among the enormous mounds of domestic refuse, the foundations of over one hundred and fifty settlements which had all been founded long before the Achaeans came. These settlements had no walls although they were many times larger than a town. From this we can tell that the inhabitants were men of peace, who lived by tilling the soil and raising cattle, fishing and hunting.

In the fourth and third millennia B.C. there were extensive forests and an abundance of good agricultural land in Greece. Wherever the immigrants settled, one could make a living.

Their leaders were given a place in Greek legend. So it is not surprising that the oldest of the Greek Kings, even the founders of Athens and Thebes, should have barbarian names. 'Barbarian' in this context means simply 'non-Greek'. Thucydides the famous historian of Ancient Greece describes an illuminating incident about the Pelopennesian War in his book. In the year 426 B.C., on the island of Delos which was dedicated to Apollo there was a purification ceremony which involved the digging up of old graves. Thucydides was present and watching closely, he made an important discovery. He knew much about the customs of other lands and it struck him forcibly that the dead, who had lain for centuries in these graves on Delos, had been fitted out like the dead of the Carians, a people of Asia Minor. Thucydides drew the correct conclusion from this. The earliest inhabitants of Delos, like the earliest inhabitants of the whole of Greece, must have come across the sea from the east.

But where then did the Achaeans come from, the 'original' Greeks?

As archaeological remains show us, they did not come as conquerors either, although they were a warrior race. Like the migrants from the east, they drifted towards Greece in larger or smaller groups over long periods of time at about the end of the third and the beginning of the second millennia B.C. According to the experts, they came from the north, from the lands around the Danube, making their way southward. And since they had good weapons, the settlers already there joined forces with them and they shared fields and forests, although they still claimed that they had lived in the land since "before the birth of the moon."

The Achaeans knew nothing of ships, but they came with their horses. They brought the Greek language with them, and that is proven by the inscribed clay tablets which were found in Pylos, Mycenae and other Achaean settlements. In the course of the following centuries, their language was adopted by the people of eastern origin too.

That the Achaeans came from the north is confirmed by the gold masks of Mycenae, for their features are neither Asiatic nor Africans. But they reveal their northern ancestry principally through their citadels, where the most important part of the building is the king's hall, the *megaron*. From it sprang the Greek temple, which we think of as typically southern. The original form that Schliemann found in Mycenae and Tiryns, and Carl W. Blegen uncovered in Pylos, makes it quite clear that it was introduced from colder latitudes.

Opposite: Cretan woman in national costume. Canea

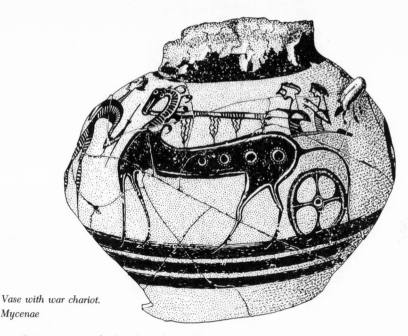

Vase with war chariot.
Mycenae

The center of the king's hall is the big round hearthplace. Around it the men used to assemble to feast, to listen to songs about the heroes, and to sit in council. They sat "within around the fire", like the Vikings and the Goths, and not out of doors in the open air as southerners do. The hearth whose glow lightened the darkness of the long evening, was sacred to the Achaeans. Whoever sought sanctuary there was inviolable. The king's hall was filled with firelight and smoke. A 'wicked' man was one who possessed neither house nor hearth, and anyone not 'steeped in smoke' was a vagabond. There was hardly any lower degradation than this for an Achaean.

The Achaeans were tough people, gifted and eager to learn. In many ways, the 'easterners' showed themselves to be superior at first. For instance, they produced more delicate pottery, they were better goldsmiths and cabinet makers. But the northerners soon caught up with them. Much for them was completely new and difficult to understand. When they had traveled to the

Opposite: Cretan man, aged ninety. Khora Sfakion

farthest point south, they came to a flat, shining surface which reached to the sky, something they had never seen before. The sea was unknown to them. They scooped up the water with their hands, sipped it and spat it out because it tasted so unpleasant. "What is this?" they asked the coast dwellers. "Thalassa", the fishermen answered them, and because the Achaeans had no word for salt water in their language, they adopted it and it became an exceptionally important word for them.

For the light that shone over shore and sea was of great magic. It tempted these northerners who had come such a long way with their horses to travel farther still. For horses of flesh and blood, with hoofs and nostrils, that was impossible, so they built wooden horses, they built ships. And there too, as in many other things, it was the easterners who were their teachers. The Achaeans however, soon outclassed them on the seas as well and they became the most daring mariners in the Aegean.

It was roughly in 2000 B.C. that they came to Greece. By about 1600 B.C. they had become the masters and built their Cyclopean fortresses. Then they went on to conquer the sea. And their god Poseidon, who was originally a god of horses, changed into a god of ships and waves. From a deity who makes the earth shake with the hoofs of his invisible steeds, he became one who plunges his trident into the sea and churns it up, a god who hurls the lightning and makes fountains rise. The horses he rode now had crowns of foam instead of manes. The sea was his empire.

But he remained a god of the Achaeans, a Greek god. An old myth tells how Athene, the goddess with the Asiatic name, fought with Poseidon, god of the northerners, for the possession of Athens. Athene was victorious over the god of horses, but she generously allowed him to take his place by her side on the Acropolis.

In the language of the historian, that is, originally it was the easterners who ruled in Greece. Then came the northerners, and the two peoples settled down side by side. The myths from earliest times tell how it began. Later the Achaeans became the undisputed masters, and the easterners were so completely absorbed that Poseidon graciously allowed Athene to share the throne on the Athenian Acropolis.

There is another ancient Poseidon legend which tells of the fall of Troy. Poseidon, so the story goes, had built a large portion of the walls of Troy for Laomedon, the son of King Tros, but he cheated Poseidon and refused to pay the sum he had promised him for it. The god was offended and planned his revenge. So when the Trojan prince, Paris, abducted the beautiful Helen, and the Achaeans set off to bring her back and wipe out the insult, Poseidon went with them and played the decisive role in the end.

For ten years the Achaeans laid siege to the stronghold of Priam, grandson of Laomedon, but in vain. Then, when Agamemnon and Achilles had quarrelled and been reconciled, when Patrocles, Hector and Achilles had all been killed, at last Poseidon's hour struck. He who could move the earth and the sea, who could create islands when he flung stones in his rage, and who could shatter the coast with his trident, appeared one moonlit night outside Troy in the form of a horse. And with mighty blows of his hoofs, he breached the walls of Troy at one particular spot, the walls that he himself had built. So it was he who decided the terrible war, for the Achaeans were able to enter the town through the gap in the wall, sack the city, slaughter the Trojans and bring back Helen.

According to this tale, which is about five hundred years older than Homer's *Iliad*, it was Poseidon, the shaker of earth and sea, who brought about the destruction of Troy. What do the scholars who have dug there say to that?

Some years ago, Marinatos, one of the most eminent of Greek archaeologists, sifted all the evidence accumulated since Schliemann's day and he came to a remarkable conclusion. The escavators had established that there were nine strata in the mound of Hissarlik. Leaving out buildings of minor importance, one can distinguish nine cities each built on the ruins of the previous ones. These different cities may be classified as Troy I–IX, with the earliest one at the bottom.

Misled by the gold he had found, Schliemann had declared that Troy II was Homer's Troy. Dörpfeld, who continued excavating after Schliemann's death, eventually came to the conclusion that it was not in the second stratum but the sixth, that one had to look for Homeric Troy. For the walls of Troy VI are as alike as brothers to the walls of Mycenae and Tiryns from which the conquerors had set out. And since calcined rubble was found in both strata, it was right to deduce that both cities had been destroyed by violence. Then, fifty years after Schliemann, an American expedition under the leadership of Carl W. Blegen began to excavate Troy. They dug there for seven whole years, using the most modern methods, and because they were a team with first class professional training, nothing escaped them. At the end of their investigations they announced that it was Troy VII, not Troy VI that had to be regarded as Homer's Troy. Troy VI must have been destroyed by an earthquake whereas Troy VII on the contrary, had undoubtedly come to its end through a war, which had taken place about 1250 B.C. or a little later.

Blegen and his colleagues have had their conclusions confirmed by the most recent research. Troy VI was indeed destroyed by an earthquake and Troy VII by a war, as they had said. The Americans had observed the facts correctly, but—they had drawn the wrong conclusions from their findings. For the war that sacked Troy VII, according to Marinatos, cannot possibly have been a war of the Achaeans against the Trojans. Troy VII was not built until after 1250 B.C. At that time, the Achaeans themselves had their hands full, trying to fend off the powerful Dorian invaders from the north. And it was these Dorians who not only threatened Mycenean strongholds, but who also destroyed Troy VII.

About 1250 B.C. all the fortresses of the Mycenean kings were reinforced. A number of refuge citadels were built whose walls were several miles long. At that time, it was impossible for the Achaeans to leave their own country undefended for ten whole years to lay siege to a city in another part of the world. But fifty years before, as the excavations of early settlements have revealed, even the wine merchants had their warehouses and shops outside the city walls of Mycenae, so small was the threat to Achaean cities in the period about 1300 B.C.

During this period, Troy VI was still standing. And it was against this Troy that Agamemnon, Odysseus, Achilles and all the rest of Homer's heroes set out on their Trojan campaign. Neither in the *Iliad* nor the *Odyssey* is there any mention that Troy was actually stormed. In Homer's version, Troy fell in the end be-

Plan of Troy I (shaded), II (white), VI (black). A Megaron; B South gate; C West gate, later walled up; D South gate; E East gate; F North bastion with cistern.

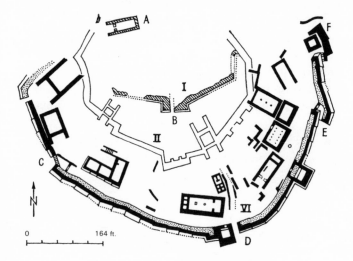

cause part of the wall was breached to allow the wooden horse to enter. As in the ancient myth, a horse plays the decisive role, only the poet attributes the main cause of victory to a man, the cunning "Odysseus of the nimble wits," and not to a god. Why is that?

One must bear in mind that it was more than five hundred years since the fall of Troy when Homer celebrated the event in words. For centuries past, the bards had sung of the Trojan wars, but every minstrel had reshaped the poem afresh, in tune with the spirit of his times. The Greeks to whom Homer declaimed his *Iliad*, could no longer know what had really happened from eye witness reports—that is, that only an earthquake had made it possible for the Greeks to invade the citadel of Troy, that the Greeks were already thinking of packing up for home when the Earthshaker came to their assistance, so that they could fall upon the stricken city and deal its death blow. Every now and then Homer allows these facts to emerge quite clearly through the narrative. But he knew what his listeners expected of him: That a Greek hero should, on the advice of a god, bring about the fall of the enemy's town by means of a cunning military stratagem. And so Poseidon's horse became the wooden horse of Odysseus.

This is a remarkable transformation admittedly, but it is no way more astonishing than that the gloom-filled king's hall of the Achaeans should turn into the Greek temple as we know it, a building flooded with light, whose pediment bears the command: Know thyself!

It needed a whole century of excavation and research before there emerged a clear picture of the rise and fall of Troy, that most renowned of all cities.

86

Troy and the Man who found it

When Schliemann had dug Troy right down to bedrock, he was deeply disappointed and wrote: "I am extremely sorry that I have to present such a small plan of Troy. Indeed, I wish I could have made it a thousand times larger, but the truth must prevail."

Schliemann could not have known that it was the plan of Troy II that he was publishing, only one of the antecedents of Homeric Troy, and that this had been built in the middle of the third millennium B.C. on the ruins of Troy I, which was older still. There was room for at most two or three thousand people within the walls of Troy II. The outer fortification walls were built of rough, unwrought stones, wooden beams and clay bricks. They were anywhere from sixteen to thirty three feet thick and on average nine feet high.

The hall in the royal house had a ceiling of cypress beams and a big circular hearthplace in the center. The Trojan people at that time lived in simple houses roofed with timber or thatch. This does not quite tally with the descriptions of Troy in the *Iliad*.

Certainly the rulers of the city were not poor. They owned gold mines not far away and they traded merchandise. Ceremonial axes that Schliemann found, indicate trade with southern Russia, where axes of jade and lapis lazuli have been found that could have been made in the same workshops as the Trojan ones. Amber jewelry from the stratum of Troy VI is evidence that there must have been communications even with the Baltic countries.

As far back as the period about 2400 B.C., Trojan goldsmiths had mastered the intricate process of granulation. For this, the craftsman drips molten gold onto a golden object, allowing tiny beads to form on the surface. In order to make sure that the article does not lose its outline in the process, the gold to be used for these drops is mixed with charcoal, thereby lowering its melting point. The golden granules then make a bond with the object without melting the surface. Granulated vessels and jewelry are particularly fascinating and probably the Trojans learned the technique from the Land of Ur.

Among the merchants who set out to travel the long roads to the plains of Troy there must have been artists and craftsmen too. Beautiful copper vessels, beaked jugs and vases with faces on them are all evidence of this.

In Troy II, there were paved streets and squares, water tanks and warehouses. From the earliest times, the princes of Troy were no "shepherd kings," but merchants and seamen who had few qualms about relieving foreign ships of their cargo now and again. For their stronghold, they had sought out the most favorable site imaginable. Troy stood at the crossroads of important trade routes by land and by sea.

The potter's wheel was already known and the utensils, weapons and ornaments that the early Trojan potters and smiths left behind them arouse our admiration.

It was not, then, the Achaeans who were present when Troy II went up in flames. It was destroyed about 1900 B.C. by the Hittites and they did the job thoroughly. The calcined stratum of ashes, slag and rubble measures more than six and a half feet in depth. Troy was razed to the ground, right down to the foundations of the city walls. It was below a section of these walls that Schliemann found the "Treasure of Priam."

In the four centuries that followed, Troy was rebuilt three times. Troy III–V had no fortifications worthy of the name, only small gateways and towers. In these strata there was no evidence found to suggest that the cities were destroyed by violence.

The houses there were modest. The largest room discovered measures only twenty three feet by fifteen and there were but few indications of prosperity.

From the bones of deer and other game, we may conclude that there was plentiful hunting at that time around Troy and the land was cultivated in the plains. But the commanding city at the intersection of important trading highways, had dwindled into a provincial backwater.

Then, about 1500 B.C. warriors from Thrace came swarming

Seal with ibex, hunter and dog

down in droves. They crossed the Hellespont and took possession of the hill of Troy in a surprise attack. Like the Achaeans to whom they were distantly related, they brought horses with them. Troy VI is the oldest stratum in which horses' bones were found in the hill of Hissarlik.

And like the residences of the Achaean princes of Mycenae, Pylos, Athens and Ithaca, Troy too was now given a fortified acropolis, nine hundred eighty four feet long and eight hundred twenty feet wide. The fortress was terraced and rose in four narrowing concentric circles. As in Tiryns or Orchomenos, the outer wall was built of Cyclopean blocks. Troy VI was equipped with three mighty gateways, several watch towers and a secret sally port. All the features that belonged to a Mycenean palace could be found here as well.

Wells were dug deep into the very heart of the hill. In the royal dwellings which were built of well trimmed limestone blocks, there were spacious rooms with floors of hard baked quicklime. In the storehouses there were "Ali Baba" crocks of earthenware almost six and a half feet high. In many of these the American expedition found there were still grains of wheat; in others there were peas, no less than four hundred pounds in one jar alone. It was in the stratum of Troy VI that Dörpfeld discovered "the broad street that ran around the town within the walls," mentioned in the *Iliad*. And what was more, there was one particular detail that establishes the case beyond any doubt. Only the surrounding walls of Troy VI have that one noticeably weak spot, mentioned specifically by Homer, although it must have been the work of mortal man and not of the god Poseidon.

Unhappily, a great part of the remains of Troy VI fell victim to Schliemann's impatience to dig right down to rock bottom as quickly as possible. Unknowingly he ordered about one quarter of Homer's city to be carted away as rubble when he dug his north-south trench.

What was left of the mound when he had finished presented a chaotic sight. This weighed on his mind and he wrote on June 17, 1873: "Unfortunately in 1871 and 1872, as a result of my mistaken notion that Troy must be sought in the deepest stratum, a great part of the city was destroyed by me; for at that time, whenever the housewalls among the upper strata of debris stood in my way I had them demolished. But this year, once I was firmly convinced by the clear evidence that Troy was not to be found at the bottom, but some twenty three to thirty three feet above, I had no more housewalls dismantled in this stratum. The most valuable masonry, such as the slabs of the path leading from the Scaean Gate to the plains was all preserved as well as the big watch tower, and there is not a single stone missing from the Scaean Gate itself."

Only it so happened that the gate that Schliemann believed was the Scaean Gate was, in fact, part of Troy II and not an entrance to Homer's city. All the same, Schliemann was justified when he stated: "The truth means more to me than anything else, and so I am pleased that my excavations of the past three years have in fact uncovered Homeric Troy, even if only to a limited extent, and I have, therefore, proved that the *Iliad* is founded on actual fact."

This was his real aim, which he had dreamed of even as a child, and which he had achieved in an endeavor that remains unique in the history of archaeology.

Schliemann was not a man to rest on his laurels as long as there were still unsolved problems. After wearisome negotiations with the Turks, he obtained a new *firman* from the very same Minister who had branded him a swindler. This permit gave him permission to continue the excavation of Troy.

Prime Minister Gladstone, his great friend in England, had introduced him to Virchow, the famous anatomist and anthropologist, and they went out to Troy together. With Virchow to advise him and profiting too from the experience of his first dig, Schliemann now excavated much more wisely than before.

Seven strata emerged clearly, and the hill of Hissarlik never failed to produce the unexpected. All the same, Schliemann and Virchow together investigated another fourteen mounds in the Troad, to see if they concealed some prehistoric city.

The previous year, a farm near the mound had been attacked by brigands, so this time, Schliemann provided himself with a bodyguard of eleven giants armed with flintlocks. Three at a time, they took turns riding behind him every morning when he went down to the sea before sunrise to bathe. Each time they received an extra payment of sixty pfennigs.

Seven strata! And still Schliemann was not satisfied. In May 1881, after Bismarck had procured yet another permit for him, he rode through the Troad on horseback, looking for Trojan settlements. He climbed Mount Ida, "the mother of wild beasts," and from a marble block—the one he believed was the throne of Zeus—he gazed down on the mound below which looked like a disturbed ant hill. And he went on digging in Troy.

Dörpfeld had been with him since 1882. In spite of stubborn opposition from the artillery commander of a nearby fortress, in spite of the overseer Bedder Effendi, who refused to allow Dörpfeld to make an accurate survey of the mound of Hissarlik, in spite of a plague of locusts and the onset of violent gales, they produced a number of excellent maps that laid the foundations for all future research on Troy.

Although Dörpfeld—whom Evans, by the way, called "Schliemann's greatest discovery"—was many years younger than Schliemann, he became more and more his teacher. It is his influence more than anything else that we have to thank for the fact that the enthusiastic amateur who set off in search of Troy developed into a serious and thoughtful archaeologist, ready to see and to admit his errors. In 1890, Schliemann bowed to the evidence that Dörpfeld had produced and conceded that Troy VI must be regarded as Homer's Troy and not Troy II. Therefore the gold of Troy could not have been the "Treasure of Priam."

Later, Dörpfeld continued Schliemann's work on the hill of Hissarlik with astonishing results. (During the First World War, the remains of this hill were destroyed by shellfire from a British warship, the *Agamemnon*.)

Schliemann's last service to the history of Troy was to summon two congresses there on the site of the excavation. He bore the cost of these himself, although he had already defrayed the expenses of the excavations themselves out of his own pocket. At these congresses he defended his work and his views against the opinions of scholars who were still reluctant to part company with their cherished prejudices.

During the year of the second congress, Schliemann undertook more traveling, but he intended to be home in Athens for Christmas, to be with his wife and children. An agonizing ear condition set in, but he was far too careless of his health, which was already impaired. Although an operation incision had not healed properly, he took a train from Halle in Germany through Italy and he was so absorbed in a book in Arabic, that he simply did not notice how ill he had become.

So he never saw his house again, nor his children, nor Sophia who had accompanied him on his archaeological ventures. On Christmas Day, he collapsed in the Piazza della Santa Caritá in Naples.

He was so humbly dressed that he was mistaken for a pauper, but when a doctor examined him and found a purse on him filled with gold, he was carried to a hotel. He was fully conscious and he gazed at the strangers who were trying to help him with staring eyes like those of the Mycenean masks. He was paralyzed. And he, a man who had mastered eighteen languages, was incapable of uttering a single word in any of them.

A few hours later, Schliemann died.

One of the most astounding men of his time departed with his death. His career was unprecedented. He had started as a penniless boy from Ankershagen and had become a multi-millionaire, so that in his prime he could use those millions to achieve a discovery as great in its way as that of Columbus.

Guided by his faith in Homer, this "outsider" had brought to light a civilization which had been relegated to the realm of fable by the experts. Since Schliemann's excavations, archaeology is "a whole continent the richer."

Schliemann had begun his work as a treasure-seeker and had in the course of his prodigious labors become a scholar to whom science is indebted for his amazing insight. Nothing could divert him from carrying out his plans. Once in Corfu, the Land of the Phaeacians, when he was looking for the spot where Nausicaa had come upon Odysseus, he discovered that he was cut off from the place by irrigation ditches and a broad marsh. Schliemann did not hesitate. He took off his clothes and in spite of all obstacles, he waded through the water in order to reach his goal.

He crossed the Dardanelles one night to examine a burial mound in a military zone. By the time the commander of the fort had discovered him and sent him packing, Schliemann had already found out all he needed for his purpose. He was a tireless man of action, yet he had time for many things. On one occasion the Emperor of Brazil visited the excavations in Mycenae, and at the end of his tour, he gave forty talers to the police officer who was responsible for his safety and asked him to dole out the money among his men. The latter suspected that their superior had been given one thousand talers, and the officer was imprisoned for embezzlement. Schliemann immediately took action. He asked the Emperor, who had gone on to Egypt by this time, to send a telegram confirming that he had given his

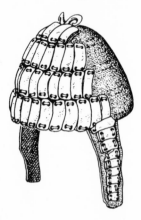

Boar's tooth helmet,
reassembled from fragments. Mycenae

friend the commandant "forty talers and not one thousand"—which the Emperor did.

There are hundreds of anecdotes like this in Schliemann's life. Sophia, whom the Archbishop of Athens had selected to be his bride, was a seventeen-year-old peasant girl. As in the fairy tales, Schliemann put three questions to her, two of which Sophia answered very wisely and the third a little too honestly. She said that she wanted to marry him because her parents had told her it was out of the question to refuse such a rich man. Schliemann rebuked her for this for several days—and then he married her.

Schliemann was Fortune's spoiled darling, but he repaid all his debts to her. He had a will of iron, and when it came to fighting obstacles, he showed the indomitable tenacity of an Achilles. So he achieved almost everything he undertook, even if the whole world conspired against him. Only once did the excavator of Troy and Mycenae overplay his hand, and it was this miscalculation that robbed him of a third empire.

On January 1, 1889, he wrote in a letter: "I should dearly like to conclude my life's work with one great achievement— the uncovering of the prehistoric palace of Knossos in Crete."

In the spring of that same year he paid two visits to Crete in order to buy the hill of Kephala, in which, according to his opinion, the Palace of Minos lay hidden. For he had a shrewd inkling of the magnitude of this new task and he wanted to begin it on land he actually owned.

But Schliemann was growing old. He was not an easy man to deal with and his increasing deafness made him more and more suspicious. He was convinced that he was an extraordinary person whom no one appreciated, or at least, that the world did not give him sufficient backing for his grand schemes. At the same time, he felt himself threatened by some insidious illness. He saw evil omens everywhere. If Sophia dreamed of crows, beanpoles or visitors from abroad, he felt uneasy. What he preferred most was to have nothing at all to do with the people around him, but to commune only with Homer, with Achilles and Agamemnon. He was reluctant to take seriously the claims of the farmer who owned the hill of Kephala. Why, he fumed, the fellow was demanding one hundred thousand francs, an outrageous amount. Schliemann was ready to pay him forty thousand. Still, the deal was almost closed when it occurred to Schliemann to check the number of olive trees that grew on this extensive site. There should have been two thousand five hundred trees. When they were counted, there were only eight hundred and eighty eight. Schliemann declared he would not deign to have anything more to do with a man who could cheat him out of one thousand six hundred and twelve olive trees and he left the country, furious.

And so it was left to another man with the necessary means at his disposal, to become the excavator of the wonderful world that lay buried in the hill of Kephala.

Clay tablet
with labyrinth sign. Pylos

Opposite: (Above) The Throne of Minos, Knossos
(Below) Cycladic steatite vase, probably representing a granary. I. of Me

Part Two

EVANS AND THE KINGDOM OF MINOS

The Collector of Sealstones

In the year 1882, Schliemann had just returned to his house in Athens from his ninth visit to Troy, when he received a visit from a thirty year old Englishman whose father was a well-known antiquary. The Englishman's name was Arthur Evans and he was accompanied by his young wife, Margaret. While Sophia talked to Margaret, Schliemann showed his guest the archaeological treasures he kept in his house. He grew very excited as he spoke about Troy, Mycenae and Homer, carried away by the pictures in his mind's eye. Evans listened attentively. Then Schliemann took him and his wife to the museum where the rich finds from the shaft graves of Mycenae were displayed, the golden masks, the gorgeous weapons and the gold vessels.

Evans observed everything meticulously, but what interested him most were the small objects, like the delicately carved sealstones and gold signet rings. Since he was extremely near-sighted, he had to hold the seals very close to his eyes, but when he did so he could see the detail as sharply as other people do only when they use a magnifying glass. He studied the markings a long time, until he knew them by heart.

It was a great moment in the life of the young Englishman.

Opposite: (Above) Bull-leaping fresco, Knossos
(Below) Sarcophagus painted in fresco technique. Hagia Triada

He had already seen seals on which there were trees, people, animals and mysterious signs, and they had at once suggested to him that they might in fact be a form of picture writing. These seals from the Mycenean graves seemed to speak to him so eloquently that he felt sure he had before him pictographic inscriptions in a language whose meaning had long been forgotten. He resolved to stake all he had on deciphering it.

Not that Evans discussed this with Schliemann. This ". . . spare, slightly built man—of sallow complexion and somewhat darkly clad—wearing spectacles of foreign make, through which . . . he had looked deep into the ground," seemed slightly sinister to Evans, who loathed glasses. And the effusive way in which Schliemann spoke of his discoveries was distasteful to the Englishman. Yet, as he left Schliemann's house, he felt strengthened in his intention to dig for himself.

Evans had already met Schliemann once before at a decisive point in his life. To celebrate their engagement, he and Margaret had visited the exhibition of Trojan finds, which Schliemann had arranged in London in February 1878. Nowhere were his deeds of discovery so loudly acclaimed as in England, once Gladstone, who was a classical scholar as well as Prime Minister, had paid Schliemann handsome recognition.

Arthur Evans was some thirty years younger than Schliemann. Schliemann happened to be in California in the thick of his adventures with gold dust the year that Evans was born. Unlike the boy from Ankershagen, Evans had been most carefully brought up and was very well educated. His father was a wealthy man and a scholar who was an expert on prehistory and geology. As a child, Arthur had played among crates in which paleolithic tools and other finds were stored. His study was a turret room from which the young man could look out over seven countries. Learning came easily to him and he gained distinction in a number of different fields.

He had been near-sighted since childhood but he soon discovered that "he could see small objects held a few inches from his eyes in extraordinary detail while everything else was a vague blur. Consequently the details which he saw with microscopic exactitude, undistracted by the outside world, had a greater significance for him than for other men." So writes his half-sister Joan in the book she wrote about her brother.

Evans loved books but he did not shut himself away in an "ivory tower." He rode and swam a great deal and was still very young when he explored foreign countries which attracted him, especially the Balkans. He was a dedicated scholar, yet adventure lured him more and he was not afraid even to risk his life if, in so doing, he could hope to achieve his aim. He was extremely self-willed and he looked for paths that no one had trodden before him. The fact that his father had a reputation as a collector made him determined that he would not become one at any price and he was greatly embarrassed when his father made him presents of Stone Age weapons and tools.

Ragusa was the place he most wanted to live in. He was passionately concerned for the small oppressed nations ground as they were then by the great powers as between millstones. In Bosnia or Herzegovina, he felt at home. But he also took a close look at other countries, Rumania, Bulgaria, Sweden, Finland and Lapland. As soon as he had finished his studies at Oxford and Göttingen, he went back to Bosnia which was fighting for its freedom.

During one of the insurrections, he and his brother Lewis were arrested as Russian spies. When they were released, unharmed, Arthur remained in the troubled area, wrote a book about the heroic sufferings of the downtrodden Balkan peoples and sent it to Prime Minister Gladstone, who had just written a "Forward" to a book of Schliemann's. Gladstone quoted in Parliament the descriptions Evans' had sent him of Turkish atrocities. Evans collected funds for refugees and as a newspaper reporter, he undertook such dangerous missions that his family were in constant fear for his safety. When Evans turned up at home un-expectedly on one occasion, he "had acquired a slightly insurgent expression," according to his sister, Joan.

He swam across ice cold rivers to visit outposts, he managed to enter refugee camps and even military forts, because he wanted above all else to provide eye-witness reports. In order to look as oriental as possible, he turned his cloak inside out and with the red lining on the outside, he moved about fearlessly among the Turks whom he attacked bitterly and ruthlessly in his newspaper articles.

He kept his headquarters in Ragusa. The Austrian authorities there arrested him on several occasions but he was not to be intimidated. When news reached him in Montenegro that the Oxford historian, Freeman, was in Ragusa with his daughter Margaret (whom Evans later married), he rode for seven hours without a break and then the whole of the following day, so as not to miss them.

Because he was so near-sighted and hated wearing glasses, he always carried a stick, which he nicknamed Prodger. Prodger went with him everywhere and was brought back to England when he was expelled from the Balkans for telling the truth, even when it caused embarrassment for the Great Powers. When a fresh uprising against the Austrians broke out in 1881, Evans immediately went back to join the Bosnian camp. He made a detour to Ragusa and ended up in prison again. He was found guilty of conspiring to overthrow the government and expelled once more.

It was at this point that he went back to his earlier intention of becoming an archaeologist. A Chair of Archaeology had been founded at Oxford not long before, and Evans applied for this professorship, but without success. Two years later, however, he found a post for which he was admirably suited. He was appointed Keeper of the Ashmolean Museum in Oxford. This was a post which assured him that freedom of action without which he could not live.

Evans dearly loved a fight and he had many a tussle with influential reactionaries, until he wrung from them the means to transform the Ashmolean from a half empty dusty old barn of a place into a museum worth the attention of serious students.

About this time, he uncovered a Celtic urn field in Kent and then he and his wife spent long periods abroad. Together they traveled to southern Russia, to Armenia, Bulgaria and Greece. They survived a number of dangerous adventures. During this time, Margaret kept a diary. She went so far as to record their

Bull's head with double ax.
Flattened cylinder. Knossos

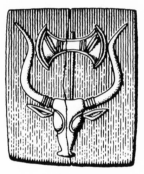

flea hunts in the dingy lodging houses where they often stayed. In two nights, they had a record 'kill' of four hundred and twenty nine fleas. Neither of them took an arrest very seriously.

The Ashmolean Museum, of which Evans was now the head, owned a large collection of coins. He was very interested in coins, and since he could read the most minute inscriptions with his naked eye, he was able to decipher the names of the artists who designed the original molds of certain Greek coins found in Sicily. From these he was able to compile a chronological table and this in turn threw a fresh light on the relationships between various Greek cities during that period.

The year 1893 was a crucial one for Evans. He was on a Mediterranean cruise with his wife when she was suddenly taken ill in Alassio. She clung to her husband's hand in agony and in a matter of hours, she was dead.

That same year, a chance encounter in Athens gave Evans the final push towards becoming an excavator. It was now eleven years since he had visited Schliemann's house and the National Museum in Athens, when he had felt strengthened in his opinion that the pictures and marks on certain seals and signet rings might be a form of writing. Since then he had collected sealstones assiduously.

When in 1889, the Ashmolean was offered a collection of similar stones, he immediately grasped the opportunity. One small red semi-precious stone, a carnelian, aroused his special interest. Evans held the smoothly polished stone close to his right eye, and he made out a number of very small engraved signs, such as the head of a wolf with its tongue hanging out, a star with four points, an arm with a dagger, diagonal crosses between two straight lines, a rams' head with one straight and one twisted horn, and a number of other and more puzzling symbols. A very early script—of that Evans was now quite sure. But what language were they in?

Evans supposed that the signs might be Hittite . . . or Syrian . . . or Etruscan. The collector from whom he bought the sealstone said that it had been found in Sparta, but Evans was certain the carnelian had been brought into the country from elsewhere, but from where? So far there were no clues anywhere.

Then four years later, in Shoe Lane in Athens, an antique dealer offered him seals with a hole bored through, and they were marked with signs similar to those on the carnelian. And when Evans asked the dealer where they came from, the man answered without a moment's hesitation, "from Crete."

The shopkeeper had given him the key to the riddle. From that day on, Evans was on the right track.

He had so many seals in his possession by now that he could draw up a list of sixty 'Cretan' pictograms. When he consulted

Impressions of the four sides of a carnelian seal. Crete

the prehistoric scholar Adolf Furtwängler, he received a further series of impressions with Cretan markings. And the famous Assyriologist, Sayce, who was an expert on antiquities from Asia Minor, showed Evans a double seal with "hieroglyphs from Crete" on it.

Evans theory brought him support from many learned men, but he found nothing that brought him a single step nearer decipherment. These mysterious signs must be so old that they went back beyond history into legend. And the language they concealed had, it seemed certain, been silent for thousands of years. In his search for the earliest possible references, Evans found a remarkable report from ancient times. It appeared that a Spartan king had found a bronze tablet during the opening of an old tomb in the vicinity of Thebes, and the tablet was covered with writing that no one could read. The Spartans sent a copy of these "hieroglyphs" to Egypt, and the reigning Pharaoh sent his priests to decipher them but they could not solve the puzzle of the secret writing. It was not very encouraging for Evans.

In March 1894, he paid his first visit to Crete. He rode on horseback across the island from east to west and he came upon the remains of at least twenty towns from very early times. He remembered that Homer had mentioned the "ninety towns of populous Crete, the island in the wine-dark sea."

He rode across one of the most beautiful islands in the world, through friendly hill country with fertile villages, where there

103

were olive trees, bananas and palms, through high tableland with thousands of windmills, along forbidding coasts, and past the deep clefts of ravines and white mountain peaks. Evans rode over hillsides purple with anemones, and fields white with narcissi or pink with wild tulips, along paths whose edges were bordered by poppies as dark as blood.

Horseback is an ideal way of traveling for anyone who wants to get to know a country. The rider is raised above ground level, yet he is not too far away from it as he would be for instance, in an airplane. He is mobile, yet he does not go too fast as one tends to by car. The horse is grateful for every halt, the rider can easily dismount and explore the immediate neighborhood. And sometimes the beat of a horse's hoof can give the excavator his first information.

Evans bought whatever finds he could from peasants and shepherds and during the following years, he continued his rovings. Most of all though, he collected 'milk-stones' which the women used to wear just after giving birth to a child, for these were charms for them and said to possess magic properties. They were very ancient and were almost always covered with mysterious markings. The young mothers could seldom bear to part with their milk-stones, but they had no objection to Evans taking impressions of them. So when political unrest forced him to leave Crete in 1896, he had at his disposal a considerable number of sealstones and seal impressions.

He met other archaeologists who had already made considerable discoveries on the island, especially the Italian, Federico Halbherr who rode an enormous black horse and had become something of a legend among the islanders. Evans had obtained rights for himself to dig on the hill of Kephala from which Schliemann had withdrawn in high dudgeon in 1890. In 1895, Evans bought part of the hill, and five years later, he acquired the rest. He had asked his father to advance him the money that would have come to him ultimately when the old man died.

The finds already made from this hill justified a demand for a large-scale excavation. In 1877, a Spanish consul had had five test pits sunk a considerable depth and had exposed the remains of a building one hundred ninety-seven feet long. Other excavators had found potsherds, remains of frescoes, a golden ring and a beautiful steatite goblet. An American, Stillman, had discovered signs of old masonry. And the Cretan archaeologist, Minos Kalokairinos had stumbled on a magazine of huge stone storage jars.

The time was ripe for the last act.

In March 1900, Evans crossed the Cretan Sea in a terrible storm. After centuries of Turkish rule, the island was now liberated and excavators no longer had to fear that either oppressors or freedom fighters would disturb them at their work. At the 'right moment', the man from Oxford set spade to soil on 'Squires' Knoll'', Kephala.

The man who had collected so many seals, hoped to find the key to the mysterious signs on them in that hill, for he was now quite sure that they were of Cretan origin.

Steatite seals. Crete

Evans Penetrates the Labyrinth

On March 23, Evans began his excavations on the hill of Kephala. He had thirty workmen to start with and three experts, David G. Hogarth, Duncan Mackenzie and Theodor Fyfe. Hogarth was eleven years younger than Evans, but he was an archaeologist with wide experience in excavation. Duncan Mackenzie had, like Hogarth, been on a dig on the volcanic island of Melos just before the turn of the century and Evans gave him the job of keeping the archaeological record. Theodor Fyfe was an architect and he undertook the tasks of mapping and sketching the sites that had fallen to Dörpfeld during Schliemann's later excavations at Troy and Tiryns.

In many ways, it was easier for Evans than it had been for Schliemann. From the very first, there were eminent colleagues to help him. Mainly though, it was due to the fact that since Schliemann's first season at Troy, methods had been developed in various places which eliminated in advance a number of sources of error. The excavations at Samothrace, which the Austrians had been working on since 1873 had set a precedent, and the excavation of Olympia under Curtius and Dörpfeld could be taken as a model.

In Crete, too, there had already been several successful excavations. The Cretan scholar Hazzidakis had achieved much in this field since 1880. At Gortyn, Federico Halbherr and Fabricius had discovered a lengthy inscription in Greek, where the laws of the city were engraved in stone. Five years later, Fabricius announced that he had found the Grotto of Zeus, three thousand two hundred seventy three feet below the highest peak of the mountain range that bears the name of Ida—like the mountain near Troy.

Greeks, Italians, Frenchmen, Americans, Englishmen and Germans had all explored Homer's "island of ninety cities" but with varying success. When Evans was making a start at Knossos, Halbherr and Pernier were already under way farther to the south, and they were soon able to announce remarkable discoveries from their own excavation.

More than anything else, Evans hoped to obtain new evidence of writing. If indeed sealstones were scattered over the whole island as his various expeditions had shown him they were, then he could certainly expect finds of that nature to come to light in the mound covering a palace. For it was from here that the ruler's commands had gone forth to the entire country.

Evans was not counting on quick discoveries. He was not impatient to get down to rock bottom immediately as Schliemann had been. Stratum after stratum was to be removed with the utmost care. It was obvious from the start that it would take years to finish the work, probably decades.

Yet within only a few days of starting, they came upon their first major discovery. It was not golden treasure that came to light as at Troy and Mycenae, but thousands of potsherds and

Clay tablet with hieroglyphs, showing a racing chariot and horse's head. Knossos

painted fragments. Amid great excitement one of the workmen extracted a small clay tablet shaped like a chisel and covered with signs, some of which looked like figures. Evans was completely convinced that this clay tablet could only have come from the palace archives. And indeed, as they dug deeper, they came to a spot where a whole collection of tablets lay side by side and they were all inscribed.

The archives of Knossos had never been plundered. Baked clay had no value for treasure hunters. But these little inscribed tiles meant as much to Evans as the "Treasure of Priam" did to Schliemann.

The painted fragments could only have been pieces of frescoes.

107

Often they were no bigger than the palm of one's hand, but the colors had not lost their luminous quality. There were birds, flowers and branches painted on them.

And then, two weeks after the dig had started, they discovered the first picture of a Cretan, a man who had belonged to the submerged world of King Minos. From two large pieces of stucco they were able to put together a life-size portrait of a slim figure carrying a slender vessel. The shoulders and the legs were missing, but all the rest was there. At first, Evans thought that it portrayed a woman, but soon it grew clear that it was a young man, pacing forth with solemn step and leaning back a little under the weight he is carrying. He is dressed in a brilliantly colored loincloth held in place by a girdle of gold and silver. On the left upper arm, he wears two silver bracelets and on his wrist there is a sealstone set with pearls. From his ear hangs a small round metal pendant. The clearly defined profile is striking with its almond shaped eyes and dark curly hair.

The color in which the body, arms and face were painted struck Evans forcibly. It seemed familiar somehow. Suddenly he knew where he had seen this reddish brown before. He recalled the reproductions he had seen of pictures from the New Kingdom of Egypt on which the "Keftiu" are represented.

The Keftiu! That was the name given to the Cretans in the Egypt of the Pharaohs. They are depicted in long processions of gift bearers, on the walls of tombs in Upper Egypt. In Qurna as in Knossos, they have the identical coloring, the same bearing and features. Evans was quite sure that this man, bearing a tall funnel shaped vessel known as a rhyton, was a Keftiu. And as Evans had discovered him in the Palace of King Minos, he called him a Minoan.

Was he one isolated figure, or had he too belonged to a whole procession?

A tiny spot of color at the edge of the fragment, only half a hand's breadth from the tall rhyton, gave Evans immediate proof that his Minoan had been one of a row of cupbearers. The spot of color was a minute portion of the upper arm of the young man in front, immediately recognizable by the remains of a bracelet that luckily had been preserved at this particular spot.

Among the Cretan workmen who had witnessed the finding of a Minoan, there were whispers of a great miracle. They took the figure to be a picture of a saint and news of the great event spread rapidly in the nearby villages. The watchman who had had to spend the night on guard by the picture, said the next morning that he had heard sounds of bellowing and neighing, and the whole site was said to be haunted.

Day after day there emerged more remnants of walls and more passages. Theodor Fyfe the architect found it harder and harder to decide what had been the layout of the palace. What had emerged was an immense confusion of corridors and rooms, in fact, a labyrinth.

The first corridor that was exposed had numerous passages from it leading to small chambers. In each of these there had once stood a man-high "Ali Baba" jar for storing oil or corn, the kind known as a *pithos*. Clearly a large proportion of the western half of the hill had once been given over to storerooms and to economic and administrative offices, which had included the two archives.

In the lowest storey, Evans discovered stone lined cysts in which, it is assumed, objects of value had been stored, for it was here that were found the remains of thin gold disks. It became clearer and clearer that within the hill were concealed the ruins of a palace of staggering dimensions and feature by feature a tentative picture began to emerge.

The buildings had consisted of several storeys with many stairways and broad terraces opening out to the east and the south. In the east wing were the royal apartments and quarters for courtiers and servants. The larger rooms had smaller ones close by, sometimes above and sometimes adjacent. The total impres-

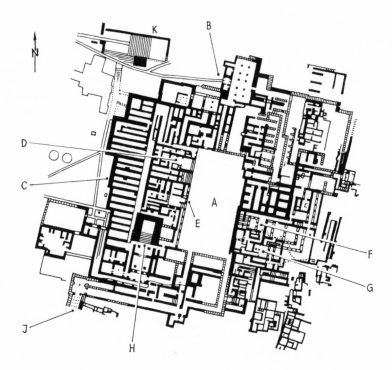

Ground-plan of Palace of Knossos. A Great Court; B North entrance with guard room; C Storeroom; D Throne room; E Small sanctuary (cf. drawing p. 166); H Hall of Pillars and entrance to royal apartments; G The Queen's apartments; H Grand staircase; I Southwest entrance; K So-called Theatral Area.

sion was of an enormous, haphazard honeycomb, a structure that had never been built to a formal plan.

The four-storeyed palace as a whole covered a surface area of about two hectares or nearly five acres. Between the east and west wings, on the flat summit of the hill, a great court had been laid out measuring one hundred sixty four feet by ninety eight.

One week after the finding of the "First Minoan" Evans discovered a room on the west side of this court, in which there stood a throne. It was not a big chamber, about twenty feet by thirteen. Along three of the walls ran stone benches and the throne stood in the center of the north wall. It was made of stone too, with a solid cube for its base and hardly any decoration at all. It had a straight back and it looked as stern as if it had been prepared for a judge of the highest court or for a god. This severity was emphasized even more by the playful, gaily colored frescoes that had once decorated the walls. From fragments, one could piece together tall lilies and griffins couchant guarding the throne.

Opposite the throne there were eight steps leading down into a small room. Here there were circular hollows in the floor, in which could be found traces of charred pillars of cypress wood. According to old legend, the king was also the high priest in the age of Minos, and so it is possible that the ruler carried out sacred rites in this lower chamber. It gives one the same impression as a chapel does.

Evans felt that the discovery of this throne room was something of a triumph for him as an excavator. After only a few weeks on the site, it was fantastic luck to have struck the very heart of the Kingdom of Minos, to have found the access to a submerged empire.

As far as the scholars were concerned, Minos, like the Trojan War, had been relegated to the realm of fable. Yet there were positive statements about him going back a long way in history. Thucydides wrote: "Minos was the first king whom we know to have had a fleet. With it, he ruled the seas which we now call the Greek Seas. He also ruled the Cyclades which he had for the most part colonized and to which he had posted his sons as governors. In order to make his enterprises secure, he had, as well as he could, cleared the seas of pirates."

Hesiod too, the ancient Greek poet, had something to say about Minos: "Of all mortal monarchs, there was none more kingly than he. He ruled over numerous tribes and held the scepter of Zeus in his hands. His dominion extended over many cities." Homer called Knossos the finest of the ninety towns of Crete. It is "the city of kings in which Minos governed, Minos who spoke with the great god Zeus every nine years." Plato too tells us in his last book, *The Laws*, that Zeus himself had instructed the first king of Crete in the art of government. Every nine years, wrote Plato, Minos had a meeting with Zeus in order to obtain advice from the Ruler of the World about how he should conduct his office as king.

A wise king, it seems then, and one who enjoyed universal respect. But how did it happen that this large island between Asia, Africa and Europe, became the seat of his power? That is a story from ancient times and it has remained for more than four thousand years in the folk memory of mankind.

In Tyros, on the coast of Asia Minor, Agenor was king. He had many sons and one daughter of great beauty who was called Europa. Zeus, the king of the gods and father of mankind, fell in love with the princess. In order to win her, he thought out a plan. He sent Hermes, the god of merchants and thieves, down to the coast near Tyros and told him to drive Agenor's cattle to the meadows, where Europa was playing with her friends. Europa noticed that the herd was led by a splendid bull, one she had never seen before. It was a dazzling white, except for a black star between its horns. He was a gentle beast and began playing with the princess. This pleased her, and she hung a garland of flowers around his horns. The bull knelt down and Europa, encouraged by the other girls, climbed on the back of the great animal and rode it down to the sea. Suddenly the bull raced into the waves. With the terrified Europa clinging to his horns, the bull carried her far out to sea. Filled with fear, Europa saw the coast of Asia sink from sight. The bull swam a long way until he breasted the surf around the rocky coast of Crete. There he came ashore and carried the princess into the mountains, to a delightful spot where there was a spring and a willow thicket, on the top of which was an old plane tree. Now the bull changed back

into a god and took Europa for his wife. She bore Zeus three sons: Minos, Rhadamanthes and Sarpedon. Zeus gave Europa a gold necklace so that her beauty would become immortal. As for Minos, the first born of Europa's sons, he was educated by Zeus himself. For nine years they lived in a cave there, for Zeus too, had come into the world in Crete, and had spent the first years of his life in a cave. His father the god Kronos, devoured all his other children, so his mother, Rhea, hid her son from such a monster. Two bears reared Zeus, a goat gave him milk, bees brought him honey and the Curetes, the spirits who lived in the ravines, rattled loudly with the shields that Rhea gave them so that the terrible father should not hear the child crying. So Zeus survived unscathed in the cave, and when he was fully grown, he overthrew his father. Then he returned to the island as king of the gods and of men, to bring up a son whom he had picked for the most exalted throne in the Ancient World. Minos was a just ruler, and his two brothers also became kings who reigned wisely. At the command of Zeus, Hephaistos forged a brazen giant by the name of Tauros, who circled the island three times a day keeping vigil. He made enemy ships keep their distance by hurling rocks at them so that Crete was secure, and it was not necessary to build impregnable walls around its palaces.

Evans found no traces of fortification walls in his excavations at Knossos. What he did find were the countless remains of splendid frescoes which had formerly decorated the spacious rooms, vessels of unbelievable delicacy, much jewelry and other signs of assured wealth. Evans found a palace kingdom that was in striking contrast to the warrior citadels of Troy and Mycenae. On the island of Minos, men lived in peace and joy, in a brilliantly colored world where there were no military fortifications—and no temples either.

None of this surprised Evans. He knew from his first rides through Crete that the earliest inhabitants of the island had worshipped their deities in shrines made by the Creator of the World himself—on mountain tops and in sacred caves.

The Secrets of the Caves

Six years before the excavations at Knossos began, Evans had ridden through the mountains of Crete with his friend John Myres, to inspect the cave that Federico Halbherr had claimed was the Grotto of Zeus. The ancient Greek geographer, Strabo, had described its location. It was southeast of Knossos and one hundred stadien, that is twelve miles, away from the royal palace of Minos. Both Myres and Evans came to the conclusion that Strabo must have underestimated the distance. The horses first had to climb uphill to the plateau of Lasithi along a poor, winding road, and then make a fresh ascent when they reached the southern side of this fertile tableland with its pretty villages, its fields and its windmills.

There lay the village of Psychro where the tempting shade of its old plane trees and its numerous springs invite the traveler to rest. Not far away, at a height of three thousand two hundred and seventy two feet above sea level, can be found the ancient cult cave. Shepherds showed the two scholars the concealed entrance.

Inside the cave Evans found a stone table used for sacrifices, with three hollows for libations. He also discovered some votive gifts and a few sealstones. It was impossible to penetrate more deeply into the cavern, though, for a great part of the roof had fallen in.

This grotto was something of a disappointment to Evans but he was able to buy several 'milk-stones' in the village, as well as the remains of a bronze tablet on which were scratched pictograms and fragments of a steatite vessel.

This was more than he could have expected, so he went away satisfied. He returned to Psychro the following two years and he learned that he could buy many finds from shepherds and farmers, which were quite useless to them but extremely valuable to an archaeologist.

Frederico Halbherr and Hazzidakis had already collected cave finds in the same way before Evans visited the region. Although the peasants at that time were mistrustful on account of the prevailing political unrest, these two men, one Italian and the other Greek, collected so many votive offerings from the cave of Psychro that they were sufficient to justify their first joint publication.

It was left to Hogarth, however, who had helped Evans start the excavation of the Palace of Minos, to lead the most important exploration of the Psychro shrine.

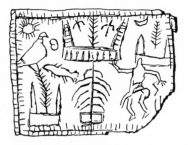

Bronze tablet. Cave of Psychro

In April 1900, when the picture of the 'First Minoan' and the throne of Minos had been discovered and the work at Knossos was progressing rapidly, Hogarth set out with a few colleagues for Psychro with the intention of investigating the cave thoroughly. He brought with him picks, explosives, axes and other equipment for excavation, and when he had gotten together a team of sixty men, women and girls he was ready to begin.

At first the girls objected to working side by side with men, for that was not the custom in Crete, especially in such a backward place as Psychro. There social customs had barely changed in centuries, and in many respects, the people still thought as they had done in the days of Minos.

But when one woman and a girl from the village had given a lead, "the ice was broken. The laughing mob brandished grain sieves and demanded all to be written (i.e. recruited) at once

116

and with their sisters, cousins and aunts, who brought up the noon meal, they made the terrace before the Cave the gayest spot in Lasithi."

The men bore holes in the rocks and started blasting until they had made an entrance to the cave from the east. Dynamiting was not without its dangers here, for across the entrance yawned an age old fissure, presumably the result of the same earthquake that had brought down the roof of the cave.

Once the debris had been cleared away, the real exploration began. Dark earth was shoveled from the floor of the grotto, and outside in the sunlight, it was shaken through sieves which caught even the smallest splinters and potsherds. The soil caked fragments were left soaking for a time in troughs of water until they emerged clean and shining.

At first, there were only five men digging inside the cave. They had to break up the hard ground with hoes and knives and twenty others piled the loosened earth into baskets and carried them out to the women and girls. Everyone enjoyed the sieving because all kinds of things kept coming to light. The girls sang as they worked and every so often there were excited cries of surprise.

They found strange objects, fragments with fishes, birds and plants painted on them, with double axes and bulls' heads, lamps, knives and ornaments. In the inmost depths of the cave, Hogarth found an altar. When he tried to dig it out, in spite of the utmost care, it crumbled to pieces before his eyes. Soon there was nothing more to be found in the upper part of the cave.

Then Hogarth decided to explore the cleft in the rock which gaped inside the cave, although he was dubious if the lower part, which was so difficult to reach, had ever been used. Down below, the black mud gleamed. A small pool gazed upward like the eye of a Cyclops.

A few of the men were roped securely and lowered one by one into the depths. "The men clambered down unwilling and not expectant, to their final task in the damp abyss, regretting the warm sunshine . . . and the girls moaned not a little at the sight of the clammy mud in which they must now stand and search."

They had no firm foothold now, and no matter how often they stooped and groped about in the slime for broken pieces, nothing but mud remained in their grasp. After several hours, even the men began to feel it was a sinister place to work in, but Hogarth had no intention of giving up. He went on searching along the floor of the cavern and encouraged the others to go on trying.

Then it happened. One of the men decided it would be better if he used both hands and he looked around for a place to rest his candle. He saw a crack in the wall which he thought would do, and as he stuck the candle in it, he touched something metallic. He looked more closely and discovered that a bronze dagger had been inserted in the crevice, and that beside it there was a broad niche. The man peered inside and saw a number of magnificently painted vases. He gave a great cry of joy and then they all stopped fishing about in the mud and concentrated on the walls and the many stalactites that hung from the roof. At first they held their breath, but before long their cries of excitement grew louder and louder. What they saw was beyond belief. Hidden in cracks and niches were literally hundreds of votive offerings, weapons, double axes and ornaments. Many of the articles had grown into the rock, for in the course of millennia they had been covered by a layer of sinter and they had to be chiseled free.

By the time this underground labyrinth had been thoroughly combed, more than one thousand finds had been brought to light.

Why, so Hogarth asked himself, had the Minoans brought their gifts into these uncanny depths to sacrifice to the divinity? The answer he found was illuminating. At that time, Hogarth was more thoroughly familiar with Crete than even Evans was, and this is what he wrote in his account: "In this most awful part of the sacred grotto, it was held most profitable to dedicate in niches that were made by Nature herself objects fashioned expressly for the god's service. In these pillared halls of unknown extent and abysmal gloom, was laid the scene of Minos' legendary converse with Zeus."

It was here, then, that the first king of the island had sought his divine father in order to obtain his advice. Hogarth had no doubt that this cave had also been the birthplace and hiding place of Zeus. "Among holy caverns in the world, that of Psychro,

Minoan stirrup vase,
painted with fishes and plants.
4½" high

in virtue of its lower halls, must stand alone," he wrote when the excavation was finished. And indeed, this cave has an unusual magic about it. To find anything comparable, one would have to examine the caves of Lascaux, Altamira or the Trois Frères, with their paintings that date from a time when mammoths and wooly rhinoceroses still inhabited Europe.

Seventeen years before the investigation of the cave of Psychro, the young German explorer Fabricius had discovered his Cave of Zeus, the Dictaean Cave. In September 1883, Fabricius was climbing in the Mount Ida range. He had heard there was a cave there in which a shepherd had made strange finds and from him, Fabricius had bought tripods, sixty gold disks and a silver brooch. When he climbed to the entrance of the cave, he found there were traces of snow which had persisted all through the summer. The front part of the cave was blocked by a thick layer of ash. From it, Fabricius unearthed a lamp from Roman times and many fragments that were much older. He found bulls' horns and when he examined them more closely, he realized that they belonged to a breed of cattle that had long since been extinct in Crete. He found too, remains of wheels and in fact, complete harvest wagons. Probably these carts had been laden with the first fruits from the fields and they had been brought to the cavern among the clouds as a sacrifice to the divinity. Today several caves have been discovered in Crete. Most of them had been looted when the archaeologists found them, as for instance the cave of Skoteino, not far from Knossos, where very little was found. From the Kamares Cave, however, which is only two hours away from Psychro, fabulous treasure was recovered.

In 1893, Hazzidakis had bought the first finds from this cave from local shepherds. In the following year, an Italian drew a plan of the sacred grotto and in 1904, an Englishman named Dawkins explored it. When he started work at the beginning of July, he had to clear away the snow from the entrance. Inside the cave, he found heaps of painted fragments, hidden away in corners. Pieced together, they made vessels of such delicate texture that one can only compare them with eggshells. And not only was the pottery itself of indescribable perfection, but so was the painting on these vases. The cuttlefish and crabs, birds and crocuses, everything that grows and moves in the sea and on the land was painted there in glowing colors. The frescoes that Evans had discovered on the walls of King Minos' palace were reproduced in miniature here in the cave of Kamares.

But by far the most productive of all the caves lies in the center of the island, not far from the ruins of the old town of Lyktos. This cave bears the name of Arkalochori. Shepherds and farmers had been extracting votive offerings from this grotto too over a long period. Various parts of it, however, had fallen in as

120   *Opposite: 'The Little Parisienne'. Fresco. Knossos*
     Inside left: Minoan vessel decorated with double axes. I. of Pseira

a result of earthquakes, and many passages were sealed off. Within these closed, subterranean chambers there lay fabulous treasure, untouched for thousands of years.

Nevertheless, it was only in 1912 when some peasants offered Hazzidakis bronze daggers for sale, that a thorough exploration of the cave was undertaken. These peasants told Hazzidakis that they had already taken a hundred pound load of such bronze finds to a scrap merchant. He had several of the blocked entrances opened and they found there bronze weapons, double axes and other objects by the thousands. Then, for a long time, silence fell on the cave of Arkalochori.

Suddenly, in 1934, there was a spate of rumors that some children playing in the cave had come upon a new cache. In great haste the local peasants made off with whatever they could lay their hands on, above all, articles of bronze. And then someone used a charge of dynamite and as a result, a certain chamber which had been shut off for thousands of years was forced open. The looters got busy immediately and hurried away with rich booty, with weapons and ornaments, vessels of gold and silver, copper bowls filled with signet rings and vases of the finest pottery to say nothing of brooches, necklaces, altar tables and lamps. The most valuable articles were double axes made of gold.

Hazzidakis hurried around, visiting all the villages in the neighborhood of the cave. A police escort helped him to put into safe keeping at least some of the plunder but most of it was lost forever. Envious neighbors were another source of information and Hazzidakis was able to swoop on certain houses and to recover among other things, twenty double axes made of solid gold or plated with gold leaf. He must certainly have felt pleased with the results of his prompt action.

Double axes were found in all the cult grottoes of Crete, double axes of copper, gold or stone, and they were painted a hundred times over on pottery or scratched on tablets. No other

Opposite: Rhyton in the form of a bull's head. Knossos
Inside right: The 'Prince's Cup', Minoan goblet. Hagia Triada

121

sign recurred so frequently, but none was more mysterious. There was no doubt that it was a religious symbol. The only puzzle was to whom it was dedicated. Presumably to the highest Cretan divinity. But wasn't that Zeus? No other god was so closely bound up with the island's legend. He had been born and brought up in a Cretan cave. He had prepared Minos, the first Cretan sovereign, for his office in a cavern there; and as a sign of his special favor to the island, he had kept it free from harmful creatures, from snakes and scorpions, even from foxes, wolves and owls.

But why, if Zeus was the most powerful Cretan god, were there no pictures of him on any of the numerous Cretan seals? On the contrary, there was always the portrait of a goddess on these. Was she the supreme divinity, "older than Zeus" and more exalted?

Among the seals that Evans found in Knossos, one preoccupied him more than the others. He himself describes it thus. "Out of five seal impressions, I was able to reproduce a wonderful religious scene; a goddess on a sacred rock or peak with two lions in heraldic attitudes on either side of her . . ."

It was almost identical with the Lion Gate of Mycenae, only in miniature. And in the center, instead of a column between the two lions, the seal has a goddess who holds a rod of authority in her hand. In both cases, the lions are leaning on their fore-

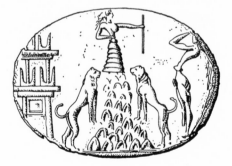

Seal with goddess flanked by lions; right, a suppliant; left, a shrine. Knossos

paws, with their heads raised, listening, as if they are waiting for the word of command.

In the Knossos seal, a man is standing in front of the goddess, looking up at her. He has raised his hand to shield his face, as if dazzled by the radiance of the goddess. Her glory strikes the suppliant with such power, that he leans back from the waist. The goddess wears nothing but a flounced skirt that looks like a bell with seven tiers. Behind her is a shrine with a roof topped with three pairs of mighty horns. Who is this goddess, standing on a mountain peak beneath the sky in such majesty and might, with a lion on either side of her? Is she a "Mistress of the Beasts?" Evans had already seen this goddess on other seals, where she appears together with animals. She rides on griffins, she rules over the fish of the sea and the snakes of the earth, or she may be accompanied by wild goats or panthers. Birds settle on her head so that their wings form a crown for her, or perhaps her hat has a snake coiled around it.

Often, however, she wears a coronet of flowers and holds lilies or poppies in her hand. On the big gold ring that Stamatakis found in the sixth Mycenean grave, the goddess sits beneath a leafy tree and priestesses bring her flowers. In the sky appears a divine child, armed with a double shield and a lance.

This divine child keeps cropping up, most notably on a ring that Evans found at Knossos. In front of a shrine, flanked by a tree and a pillar, a boy god hovers in the air. His proud bearing and his outstretched arm that holds a wand are reminiscent of the goddess with the lions, standing so imperiously on a mountain peak. Here it is she who stands before the child, whose hair is fluttering in the wind, and she looks up at him.

Almost always we find her represented by trees or flowers. Is this the goddess who makes the fields fruitful? Does she make the meadows blossom and bring forth all life from the lap of the earth? Is she the Great Mother, who was worshipped in various forms by all primitive peoples, especially those in the Orient?

Later, the explorers in Crete found more and more clues. She is the goddess of spring, associated with new life on the earth. Year after year she brings "the divine child" into the world.

It fits in with this picture that Zeus, the ruler of the world, should be depicted most often as a child in Crete for it was here that Rhea bore him in the depths of the earth and kept him safe

Isis sign and looped cross. Egypt

from the attacks of his vicious father. And since she could not always be with the child, she ordered the bears, the goats, the bees and the spirits of the earth to guard him. She mustered all her power to safeguard his life, and according to the Greek myths, she succeeded. They say that when he grew to manhood, Zeus left the island and won for himself dominion over heaven and earth. The ancient Cretans, however, believed that Zeus had never left Crete. His life remained threatened for all time. Just as Osiris of ancient Egypt died and always rose again, so Cretan Zeus died and was born anew like the flowers that wither and bloom again, like the ears of corn that are cut down and whose seeds become new ears. The cult knots which are found in large numbers in Crete are a symbol, like the looped cross or "Isis Knot" of Egypt, symbols both to the key of life.

On many Cretan seals there are strange engravings that remind one of butterfly pupae, creatures in transition, no longer caterpillars and not yet butterflies. Other pictures show pillows or sacks laced up, and inside them are human figures that have turned into chrysales. This represents the hour of initiation. After severe testing, one is allowed a glimpse into the most profound mystery of all. On the point of departure, man achieves the certainty that life does not end with death.

This faith was shared by the ancient Egyptians, the Indians, the Babylonians, and even the Ice Age Hunters. It was a belief stronger than man's actual experience, for this must have told him that he was threatened at every moment and his life might be forfeited at any time. The ancient Cretans, whose island was constantly shaken by severe earthquakes, trusted in the Great Mother, to whom all life is sacred. Like all primitive peoples, they were deeply religious.

Ritual customs are depicted on Cretan seals too. Helpful spirits are conjured up by men blowing conch horns; or demons appear in terrifying forms, as winged goats, as dogs dragging pitchers, as bird-headed men and as hippopotami with the horns of an ibex.

The significance of these images is a closed book to us. All we know for certain is that the Minoans built no temples but worshipped their gods in the open air, on mountain tops, in holy meadows and in deep caverns. In many places they erected their sacred pillars, or instead, they set up double-bladed axes several feet high.

For many races in ancient times, the double ax was a religious symbol. The child god of the Hittites carried it as a scepter. In Denmark, a splendid stone specimen of a double ax was found, probably ten thousand years old.

Cult knots. Crete

In the Palace of Minos, Evans found the double ax in many places. In one hall with squared stone pillars it occurred so often that Evans called it the "Hall of the Double Axes."

Both the Greeks and the Cretans called the double ax *"labrys"*.

This ancient word had been brought by migrants from Asia Minor long before, together with the double ax itself as a religious symbol. It is true that the Greeks at the time of the first Olympic Games had forgotten all about it. They saw the Palace of Minos only in ruins and to them the word "labyrinth" meant the same as it has done for all succeeding peoples, a maze of stone walls, from which it is impossible to find one's way out without some kind of help.

It was only at the excavation of Knossos, when no other sign appeared so often as that of the double ax that the original meaning became clear: The House of the Double Ax. For the Minoans, the Palace of Minos was not a confusion of subterranean passages with no way out, but a building flooded with light, in which lived their kings, rulers of divine ancestry, who governed the island and the seas around it so wisely that Cretans could live in peace.

Minoan double axes

Pictures of Minoan Life

When the heat began to grow unbearable in Crete in the summer of 1900, Evans, Mackenzie and Fyfe broke off the dig at Knossos for the season. Above the hill, from which they had shifted a thick layer of earth and stones, the air shimmered, as if a fire were smouldering beneath the ruins of the palace.

In February 1901, the three archaeologists returned to their work. Day after day they left the house in Herakleion which Evans was renting from a Turk, and rode on mules through the tunnel-like gateway in the fortification walls, past the lepers begging outside the town, and along the road to Knossos and the excavation site.

New stairways and passages, new storerooms, living quarters and bathrooms were uncovered. Vessels, utensils, even Egyptian statues were unearthed, but most of all they found pictures.

In the sacred caves of Crete, in which thousands of votive gifts had been deposited, not a single painted picture or carved relief had been found on the walls or in obscure corners, in marked contrast to the cult grottoes of the Ice Age hunters. But more and more paintings emerged from the hill of Knossos and their colors have the same luminous quality as the pictures in Altamira and Lascaux. The red, the yellow, the blue and the green, even the black and white of these fragments were as vivid as if they had been done very recently and not three thousand five hundred years ago.

The excavators could tell by the broken edges that the pigment had penetrated deep into the plaster, so the painters must have slapped the pictures onto the walls while the latter were still wet. They must have penciled the outlines beforehand, lightly sketching in the figures of men, animals and plants and then applied the colors so quickly that the pictures appeared as if by witchcraft. There is never the slightest sign of hesitation re-

The Queen's bathroom, reconstructed. Knossos

vealed in these pictures. They are so alive, the painters have captured the very moment of inspiration.

It was a laborious job putting together all these pictures. Many of the frescoes had been so completely destroyed when the palace walls collapsed that not all the team's patience and experience could save them. There were pieces missing in all but a very few of the restored frescoes. Even so, what remains is incomparably fascinating.

In these pictures life, as it existed for the Minoan artists, has been caught and held in a magic spell. They show landscapes suffused with light and richly peopled. Hares chase around bushes, pheasants stand among rose hedges, monkeys scamper up brightly colored rocks. There are broad surfaces covered with rushes and papyrus, with grass and flowers, with ivy and palm trees. Crocuses, irises and lilies in great profusion are woven into carpets of flowers. Deer graze in blooming meadows, wild cats lie in wait for birds, girls kneel before beds of flowers and pick the blossoms.

Opposite: (Above) Two bees with honeycomb. Gold pendant. Mallia
(Below) Vessel in the shape of a ram

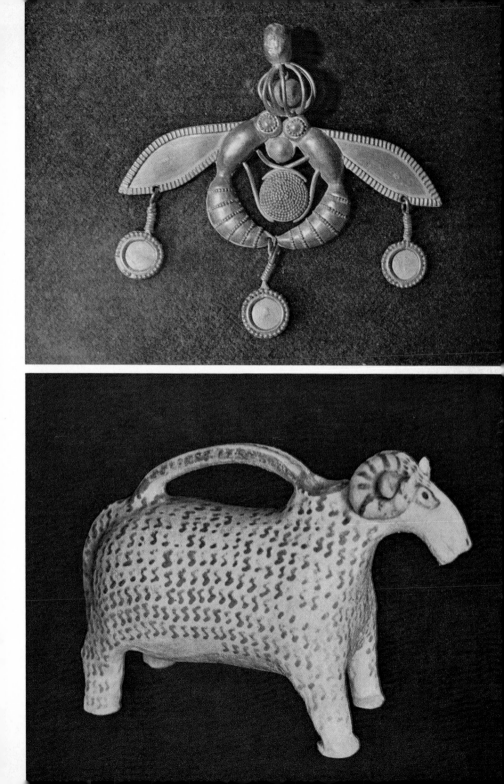

The early Cretans were passionately fond of flowers. They wanted gardens and parks with gay fountains, butterflies and bees to come inside their houses too, for they wanted spring to last throughout the year. Everything luminous and so gossamer light that it floats on air, the Minoan painters have captured a thousand times on frescoes and on pottery, articles which weigh hardly more themselves than the flowers and small birds painted on them. Evans had found in Knossos too, countless splinters of vases described as "eggshell ware." The Roman poet Ovid called them "windborne and wafer thin." The clay out of which such ceramics are made had to be wetted down and kneaded time and again for months on end to make it both pliant and durable. And from the tiny splinters, many vases could be put together again, complete with the pictures which adorned them.

The Minoan painter set the experts many puzzles too. In one of the lower stratum, not far from the Throne Room, they dug out one picture that made them rack their brains. The first piece that came to light showed a white crocus. Then two further flowers appeared and between them was a foot, painted blue.

'The Saffron Gatherer'. Incomplete fresco. Knossos

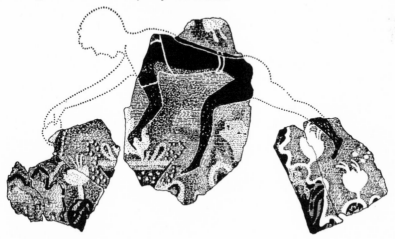

Opposite: (Above) Grand staircase, Phaistos
(Below) Pithoi storeroom, Palace of Knossos

Altogether ten fragments emerged, from which could be put together a torso, a left arm and two legs, a figure plucking crocus flowers. Evans called it "The Saffron Gatherer."

He found it a remarkable picture for several reasons. The painter had worked very boldly with crocuses growing everywhere not only in flowerbeds and pots at the lower edge of the picture, but also along the back and across the shoulders of the flower picker. But what was more surprising than anything else was the blue with which the body, arms and legs were painted. This blue was a challenge for the scholars, for on all Minoan pictures with human figures, the women are painted in white and the men a brownish red. This is adhered to rigidly, as if there were a strict rule about it.

Then Evans looked at the flower picker more closely, and he noticed that the hand could not be distinguished very clearly from the foot. Apparently it was not a human foot after all that had been placed inside the flower bed. Besides, the figure is crouching so far forward that it looks as if it were moving on all fours.

Another fresco which they found later solved the riddle for them. On this a blue figure was easily recognizable. It was a monkey. More pictures with blue monkeys turned up when they dug outside the palace confines and uncovered the remains of a house which had belonged to a wealthy man, a person of taste. The Minoans kept domestic pets, including monkeys, who took liberties everywhere, it seemed. So why not a walk through the flowerbeds!

Being islanders, the sea was a familiar subject for Minoan painters. Maritime themes occur on many jars, and painted on the walls, there are waves and flying fishes, overgrown coral reefs, starfish, polyps, shells and murex.

For the Minoans, the world did not stop at the coast of Crete. Ships brought back such abundant riches from coasts near and far, that huge storehouses were built and heaped with treasure.

Evans found copper bars, each of them weighing nearly sixty-five pounds.

Around the palace buildings, an extensive city grew up, in which it is estimated, one quarter of a million people lived. What the houses looked like is revealed by a find of several small faience tablets. Everyone of them depicts a house and they all had flat roofs and tiny windows. The door is not always at ground level. There were stone steps leading up to them, and perhaps wooden ones too. The houses were painted and on many of them, the timberwork can be seen between the mud bricks, as in Tudor houses, or in some European farmhouses even today. More than two storeys were rare for a house, but they were all packed tight like the cells of a honeycomb. In the Cretan palace communities, the inhabitants lived as close together as bees in their hive.

We see them crowded together on grandstands, sitting around an arena where games and contests take place. The men as well as the women wear a great deal of jewelry with armbands and chain bracelets around their wrists as well as earrings. Their hair is artistically arranged as if they had just come from the hairdresser's, the men are meticulously shaved. The men's clothing consists of a loincloth or kilt of some gaily patterned material and a belt. For cooler weather, they would put on a short cape as well and for traveling it was usual to wear sandals and puttees.

On ceremonial occasions the Minoans were an impressive sight. No fewer than five hundred and thirty-six life-size figures all bearing gifts were counted in a procession that Evans found in one of the corridors. Princes were drawn taller than life-size, with a crown of peacock feathers on their proudly raised heads.

The women wore close-fitting jackets, open in front, and broad skirts of precious materials. Their hair was held in place by a coronet. Neck and arms were laden with jewelry. The Cretan ladies who look down at us from these pictures are far from shy with their great dark eyes, their pert little noses, their delicate chins and lips that remind one of flowers.

The Minoans loved festivals and displays, music and dancing, table games and sporting contests. Long before the first Olympiad in Greece there were competitions staged between champion wrestlers and boxers in Crete. They were tough fighters too, as witness the helmets they wore to protect their heads.

For the excavators, these pictures came as a surprise. They had gotten to know the Minoans through their many frescoes as a people with a marked feeling for beauty, who would rather observe wild game than hunt it, who took pleasure in birds, flowers and fountains. Now it was revealed that they could fight grimly if only in sport.

Among the most exciting finds were numerous portrayals of a sport that was literally a matter of life and death. This was the bull game, where the maddened beasts were provoked to rush at young men, who deliberately stood in their path and then, at the last moment, somersaulted over the back of the charging bull.

There are frescoes showing spectators in a frenzy of excitement. They have thrown up their arms, their mouths are wide open, screaming at the tops of their voices. No doubt there were always fatal accidents and pictures on vases show how easy it was for a bull to gore a man to death. In spite of the danger, though, the bull-leaping sport was practiced in the kingdom of Minos as long as there was a palace standing in Knossos.

The bulls were bred especially for this sport, for they were dappled, and in their natural environment this would not have been the case. From two golden cups, admittedly found in Sparta, but undoubtedly made by craftsmen from Crete, we know that they were exceptionally ferocious beasts. We can see bulls being captured on both cups, but the artist shows how the outcome could vary on different occasions. One man succeeds in luring the bull into a net. The animal runs into it full tilt, actually fall-

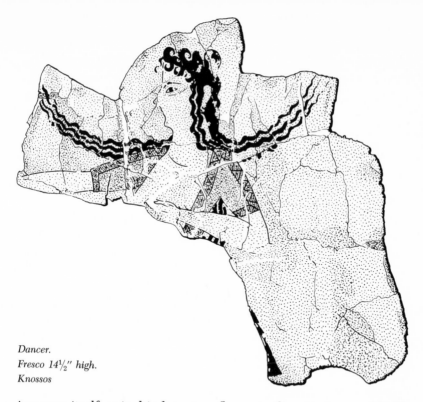

Dancer.
Fresco 14½″ high.
Knossos

ing over itself as its hindquarters fly up in the air. A second bull, however, shakes off its would-be captors. One man has slipped by the side of the bull, and he goes flying too, but down on his back while the bull gores his companion.

On the other goblet, the bull stands beside a decoy cow. He is so preoccupied with his courtship, that he does not realize what is happening to him. One hind leg is already caught in a noose. The bull catcher does not seem to be at all worried about what the bull will do when he discovers he is trapped.

Bull jumpers and bull catchers were as exposed to danger as warriors in the face of an enemy. They risked their lives every time, and what is more, they not only did it unarmed, but they had to fight monstrous brutes, not mere human beings. But there were soldiers too in the kingdom of Minos. Evans found one

133

fresco on which there are armed men, recruits from far away Africa. Negroes as mercenaries, in the Palace of Knossos! Only the leader is not a Negro. Evans called him "The Captain of the Blacks." These dark skinned soldiers wear helmets of dark fur with goats' horns. A belt and a loincloth with a striped border are their only clothes, apart from a necklace and ankle rings. Two slender spears are carried in the right hand, their only equipment, so it seems. Are these terrifying warriors going into battle? It hardly looks like it. They are advancing with dancing steps and surely no one would be sent into battle so badly armed. Probably these Negroes belonged to the Palace Guard and were intended principally for show, for ceremonial processions, when everything had to be gay and colorful.

There was a vase found by Federico Halbherr on which such mercenaries can be seen too. They march in ranks, at their head is a captain in a cuirasse that reminds one of crocodile scales. The edge of this curious armor is trimmed with fringes. The leader is shouldering a crook and eight lusty marching men follow their captain. Then comes the band. This consists of three singers, pictured with their mouths wide open, and the man in

Cretan officer, captain of the palace guard.
Knossos

front is holding up a rattle, apparently to give them the time. The singers carry shields that suggest cymbals.

The rest of them are equipped alike, each carrying a trident on one shoulder, that is, a fork with long prongs. From the handle of the fork, there is a reaping hook, like a pennon. And on the right thigh every man back of them has buckled on something that looks like a club, to hit the enemy on the head. But these warriors themselves do not look very menacing. They are marching along jauntily and one man who has stumbled is carried along by the others without a halt. Men do not usually march into battle in such a hurry where some of them may lose their lives. In fact, it seems much more like a "harvest home" procession, like a return from the olive groves. And the "clubs" are probably bottles of wine, to keep the marchers in a good humor. In no sense are these warriors Achaean heroes, as Homer describes them. With their cheerful faces, they belong to a world where peace is esteemed more highly than war.

Another Cretan find is known as "The Prince's Goblet." There are "soldiers" on this too. The Prince has dug his staff of office into the ground to signify his rank and he is listening to the report of an officer, with a waving plume on his helmet. Three figures are led forward carrying huge hides, probably elephant hides, to judge by the tails. So these are Africans bringing tribute or gifts, are they? One look at their faces explains the mystery. They are children making a game of what they have often seen. They are playing at presenting gifts to the ruler of Crete.

That the Minoans were also fond of innocent games is shown by one valuable find. It is a little clay figure of a girl sitting on a swing. The uprights have been preserved too, only the rope which once secured the seat to the posts is missing. It must have been of hemp or some similar material which has perished.

Of course there are weapons too, most of them are richly ornamented. Especially beautiful is a stone ax, shaped like a leopard, a beast of prey that looks both ferocious yet tamed at one and the same time. Nothing epitomizes the attitude of the Cretans towards war better than this ax. Savagery is transformed into power with restraint.

It is not unlike the double ax, the symbol of holiness and it is indeed highly probable that it was made as the tip for a staff of office, for a scepter in fact. It is a reminder of Minos and his successors, to whom were subject the island of Zeus and the seas around it.

Stone ceremonial ax in the shape of a leopard,
6″ long. Mallia

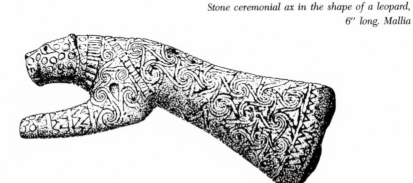

Cretan Ships Sail Far and Wide

Crete lies among three continents, set in a sea that often encircles its coasts with a girdle of surf. Whoever approaches the island from the south or the east comes face to face with a fortress whose forbidding walls are of solid rock. The pinnacles of Mount Ida, the Lasithi Mountains and the White Mountains tower like battlements more than six thousand five hundred sixty feet high.

The Cretans had the choice of either turning their backs on the sea for good and living on their secure island, or of showing their prowess as sailors. As they had arrived by ship, they decided to go on farther across the seas and to make for foreign shores. They built ships with a high prow and sailing masts, and thirty oarsmen on either side made them independent of the winds. In the roomy holds, there was ample space for cargo.

Where did these Cretans travel?

What were the goods they offered?

Where did they obtain their imports?

Beneath the paving of the great palace court at Knossos, Evans found a strange little statue. It was made of diorite and showed a man seated. The inscription on the statue was in Egyptian.

An alabaster lid came to light too, and this was also inscribed with Egyptian hieroglyphs. It bore the name of one of the Pharaohs, Chian. He belonged to the Asiatic Hyksos people who conquered Egypt and ruled the country between 1700 and 1600 B.C.

A whole range of alabaster ware was discovered in a rock chamber tomb not far from Knossos. And it was not only in the palace of Minos and the surrounding countryside that these things came to light. Throughout Crete were found vessels, jewelry and utensils which had been brought from Egypt. The peculiar rattle on the vase with the singing mercenaries, who are going out to the harvest or returning from it, is a sistrum, an Egyptian musi-

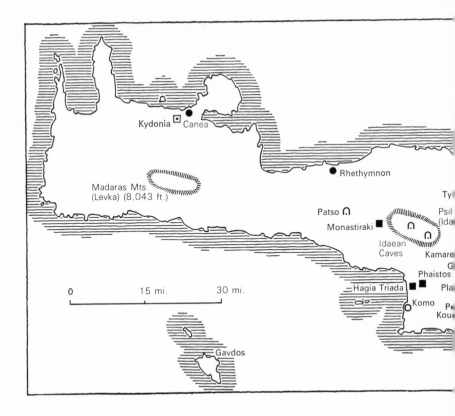

Kydonia □ ● Canea

Rhethymnon

Madaras Mts.
(Levka) (8,043 ft.)

Ty

Patso ∩

Psil

Monastiraki ■ ∩

(Ida

Idaean ∩
Caves

Kamare

G

Phaistos

0   15 mi.   30 mi.

Hagia Triada ■ ■

Pla

Komo   P
Kou

Gavdos

cal instrument. In return, many articles from Crete have been
found in the land of the Pharaohs. In the grave of the Pharaoh
who drove out the Hyksos, for instance, there lay among other
objects a sword of state decorated with lions, their legs outstretched, running. At that time, it was only on Minoan weapons
that we find lions in such attitudes. Weapons from Crete were
much sought after in the land of the Nile, but it was Minoan
pottery more than anything else that was shipped to Egypt. In
many tombs in the New Kingdom there have been found vases,
jugs, cups and dishes just like the ones discovered in such abun-

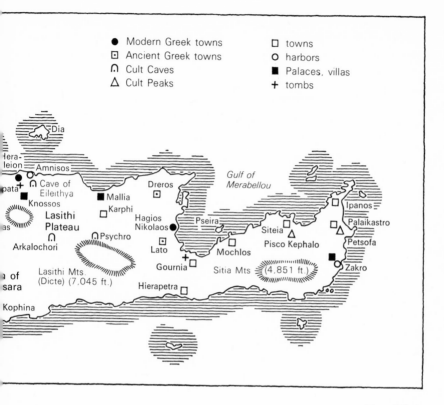

Legend:
● Modern Greek towns
⊡ Ancient Greek towns
∩ Cult Caves
△ Cult Peaks
□ towns
○ harbors
■ Palaces, villas
+ tombs

Dia
Hera-leion
Amnisos
Cave of Eileithya
pata
Knossos
Lasithi Plateau
Arkalochori
Psychro
a of sara
Lasithi Mts. (Dicte) (7,045 ft.)
Kophina
Mallia
Karphi
Hagios Nikolaos
Lato
Gournia
Hierapetra
Dreros
Pseira
Mochlos
Sitia Mts.
Gulf of Merabellou
Siteia
Pisco Kephalo
(4,851 ft.)
Ipanos
Palaikastro
Petsofa
Zakro

Map of Crete

dance in the cave of Kamares and in Minos' palace, "eggshell ware, wafer thin and floating on the breeze."

Inscriptions tell us that embassies from Crete brought silver rings, baskets filled with lapis lazuli, ceremonial vessels shaped like the heads of animals, lions, bulls, griffins and goats, as well as necklaces of red and blue beads and splendid daggers. The text states that these were tribute, but that is just boasting. The Pharaohs never subdued the Cretans nor made them pay tribute.

139

Neither did the Minoans come as conquerors to Egypt. It was simply give-and-take, a lively commerce and exchange of goods between the two countries.

The Cretans brought with them cypress wood, wine and oil, ceramics, textiles, purple dye and weapons. The blades of their swords were second to none. They were reinforced by a strong midrib and they were beaten by such skilled craftsmen that they did not snap off even on impact with armor.

From Egypt, the Cretans brought back copper, tin and silver, utensils, rare timbers, faience, ivory and ostrich eggs. And golden jewelry! From an otherwise wholly destroyed fresco, Evans found a piece no bigger than a child's hand. On the right there are three fingers, painted brownish red and therefore belonging to a man. To the left, one can make out part of a chain of small gold beads from which there hang tiny golden heads. Minute as these golden faces are, they reveal their African origin. They are Negro heads wearing earrings. The three male fingers are in the act of fastening the chain by pushing a thorn through a loop. The white against which the golden necklace gleams tells us that someone is fastening this gold from the Land of the Nile around a woman's neck. That is how a tiny remnant of a picture can tell a whole story.

After the Hyksos had been driven out, Cretan trade with Egypt flourished. But even during the Middle Kingdom, in any event, after 1900 B.C., Minoan craftsmen were employed along the banks of the Nile. At the time of the New Kingdom, contacts were closer still and Minoan potters, smiths and painters, worked for the Pharaohs of the eighteenth dynasty. Minoan traders and seamen returned to Crete with not only goods but also scarabs from Egypt.

In the grave of the Treasurer of Thutmose III, an embassy from Crete is portrayed. They carry vases and ritual vessels in the shape of animal heads. The second man in the Keftiu procession is specifically described in the text as an artist.

Cartouche with the name of the Hyksos Pharaoh. Chian

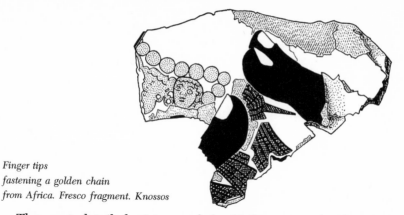

Finger tips
fastening a golden chain
from Africa. Fresco fragment. Knossos

The most detailed pictures of the Keftiu are to be found in the tomb of Sennemut. He was the confidant and adviser of Queen Hatshepsut, the only woman to occupy the throne of the Pharaohs. She detested war and won fame by working for peace. She healed the wounds inflicted on the country by foreign attacks, she built splendid temples and she organized an expedition to the Incense Land of Punt. Sennemut played a great part in all her schemes and it is quite certain that they were in particularly close touch with the Cretan kings, who had as few aggressive intentions as they.

The same can be said for Ikhnaton, the Pharaoh who broke with the practice of worshipping many gods and who saw in the orb of the sun, the life-giving sign of the one and only God and Creator.

Ikhnaton, like Hatshepsut, wanted to reign in peace. He felt a bond of brotherhood with all men. In the midst of the desert he built a town laid out with flower gardens, a paradise in which there was a place for artists as well. The town was known as the "Horizon of Aten" and today it is called Amarna. In the days of Ikhnaton, in the sculptors' studios, there were carved statues which do not give the impression of being in the strictly formal Egyptian manner but are much more natural and animated. The

141

pictures which Ikhnaton's artists painted have the luminosity of Minoan frescoes. In Amarna as in Knossos, there are vivid landscapes on the walls, with birds in flight and flying fish, with grass and flowers with the wind blowing through them.

It is quite certain that Ikhnaton had not only Egyptian artists in his palace. His closest advisers were foreigners "whom he had made into something from nothing." He had an enlightened attitude for everything foreign, and he did not discriminate between Nubians and Asiatics, Keftiu and Egyptians. In his Hymn to the Sun, which he addressed as a prayer to the one god and creator, he actually names foreign lands before the kingdom he himself ruled. In the space of a few years, a style grew up in the court of Ikhnaton, which shows distinctly Minoan features.

But Minoan ships did not sail only to Egypt. They obtained marble from Paros and Naxos, obsidian from the island of Melos, lead and silver from other Aegean islands and from Asia Minor. Nor were these cargoes invariably bound for Crete. Many harbors lay open to their ships.

Since approximately 2000 B.C., the Cretan sea trade was considerable and for a century, between 1900 and 1800, Minoan fleets ruled the Aegean Sea and the western Mediterranean as well. There was no power which could dispute their supremacy.

Cretan ships sailed out past Sicily to Tartessos in Spain, and the name of Minos was remembered there until Roman times. Vessels from Crete were found on the Lipari Isles to the north of Sicily. And a bar of bronze from Minoan Crete was fished out of a harbor on the southern coast of England three hundred years ago.

The majority of Cretan ships, however, visited Asian ports. In the Upper Euphrates among the palace archives, there were found cuneiform despatches in which it is mentioned that precious articles were brought from Knossos to the palace of Mari. The ships brought not only goods with them but ideas too. So for instance, the custom of placing a pair of sacred horns on the rooftops and of erecting the double ax, most probably came from Asia.

In recent times, the archaeologist J. Mellaart has excavated the shrine of Catalhüyük in Turkey. There he uncovered a cult room which is about one thousand years older than the palace of Minos,

Keftiu bringing gifts to the Pharaoh.
Fresco from the tomb of Rechmere. Upper Egypt

where the roofs were adorned with pairs of horns in stone. Mellaart found such horns as these in Catalhüyük. They decorated the walls of the chamber, as well as the stumps of the pillars that stood before the walls. Mellaart could produce proof that the worship of the bull which played such a significant role in Crete, goes back to the sixth millenium B.C. in the eastern part of Asia Minor.

There was barter between Asian countries and Crete in all kinds of ways. The lively exchange of correspondence between the palaces of Asia has been preserved in part and this too throws light on the relationships of the Asiatic palaces with that of Knossos. In one such letter, the King of Ugarit beseeches the King of Yamhad to obtain for him an invitation to visit the palace of Mari whose magnificence he has heard so much about. Cretan ships sailed to Ugarit as well as to Byblos.

They made their way across the open sea, for that was safer

than hugging the coasts where the reefs are so dangerous. For several centuries Cretan ships were safe from pirates so that Knossos and the other Cretan palaces flourished. The towns around the palaces grew considerably in size and the palaces themselves became trading centers.

This increasing wealth made an astonishing level of luxury possible. Baths and sewage disposal were taken for granted. Excavators discovered that the Queen's bathroom at Knossos had been converted from a living room and it was only later that it was fitted out with a bathtub and drain pipes.

Fountains were built as well as grandstands around the sports grounds where games and contests were held. For the nobility guest houses were provided and they had litters for transport. For the common people there were donkeys. The horse was a late introduction to the Minoan world.

In the so-called Little Palace, Evans found a broken seal impression whose center portion fortunately had remained intact. It shows a galley with a mast, a big ship, that is. A horse is being transported by sea and the artist has made it almost as big as the ship, so important did it seem to him. The horse's mane is tied back in flowing tufts and the ship is for its exclusive use. Evans called the impression "The Coming of the Horse." With it, Crete was on the threshold of a new era.

For the horse was brought to Crete by the same people as those who had traveled the long journey on horseback from the Danube basin to Mycenae, Tiryns and Pylos, that is, by the Achaeans. Once they had settled down in their secure fortresses, they too built ships. Since about 1800 B.C. they, like the Cretans, had sailed to Egypt, Asia and the Aegean Islands. There is no doubt that they came to Crete too. Probably they even entered Cretan service.

The Lords of Knossos were so powerful that their word was heard on every shore. Many rulers sent presents to the palace of Minos—and tribute too. There came a time when the Achaeans

Opposite: (Above) Hagia Triada, with Mount Ida in the background
(Below) Water pipes. Hagia Triada

became subject to Crete and they saw their freedom menaced by Minoan might.

This is reflected in the Greek myths which tell of Crete.

At first the Achaeans looked admiringly across the sea to the island that was governed by Minos, the son and the confidant of Zeus. For them too he was the model of a wise king. His palace was the holy "House of the Double Ax." So say Homer and Hesiod, the ancient poets of Greece, when they speak of those early days. One can read of it too in the works of the historian Thucydides.

Later poets and historians, however, tell of a Minos legend in which everything is reversed. The divine ruler has become a cruel tyrant and the House of the Double Ax, has become the cavern of a monster whom the Athenians especially thought of with the utmost abhorrence.

'The Coming of the Horse'. Seal-impression. Knossos

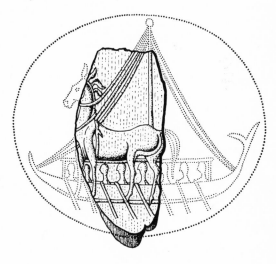

The Legend of Daedalus, Theseus and Ariadne

At the time when Minos the Second reigned over Crete, King Aegeas ruled in Athens. His palace was built on the acropolis, the upper town perched on the rocky mountain citadel.

There also lived a man named Daedalus, whose mother was of royal blood. Daedalus was equally outstanding as a sculptor, engineer and inventor. He made statues of the gods with hands and feet of ivory and he gave them golden faces of such beauty and radiance that the figures seemed to be alive. Daedalus was the most celebrated of all craftsmen.

His most gifted pupil was his nephew, a boy named Kalos, the son of his sister Perdix, which means 'partridge.' Kalos was quick to learn and it looked as if one day he might overtake his uncle in ingenuity. Daedalus surprised him one day as he lifted a snake from the floor, looked thoughtfully into its jaws at the rows of pointed teeth and then went into the workshop. There he filed teeth into a knife and so invented the saw. On another occasion he took a forked twig and by sticking one end firmly into the sand, he found he could easily describe a perfect circle with the other prong. The Master began to tremble for his reputation as the greatest inventor of his time.

And so, one night when the moon refused to light up the earth, Daedalus led his nephew to the edge of the precipice on the Acropolis, pretending he wanted to show him a newly discovered star. As Kalos raised his eyes to the sky, Daedalus pushed the boy into the chasm below. Then he fled, for he knew that a common murderer could expect no mercy in Athens. Unrecognized, he escaped to Crete by ship and Minos the Second allowed the craftsman to stay with him and took him into his service. For Ariadne, the King's daughter, Daedalus designed a playground. For the Minotaur, however, a monster half man, half bull, the offspring of Queen Pasiphae with a white bull for its father,

King Minos had a labyrinth built, a subterranean maze from which no one could find his way out without help. In the innermost recess lived the Minotaur, waiting for the human sacrifices with which Minos sought to appease him. For in his savagery, the monster in the bowels of the earth would fling great boulders against the walls of the labyrinth, so that the sound reverberated; it was terrifying to hear, and the King's palace shook.

Minos fetched the human sacrifices which he threw to the Minotaur from foreign lands. And when envious rivals killed his son at the Athens' Games, Minos demanded as compensation a yearly contribution of seven youths and seven maidens from the Athenians.

This ghastly tribute was now due for the third time when Theseus, the son of Aegeus, appeared on the scene. The Athenians did not know of his existence, for Theseus had been brought up by his mother, Aithra. She was a king's daughter and Aegeus had made love to her on his way home from Delphi. He had left his sword and his sandals for his son, hidden away beneath a great boulder. When he had grown to manhood, Theseus had rolled away the rock and on his way to Athens, he had performed a number of heroic deeds with his father's sword. Aegeus had immediately recognized him by the sword, and when he heard of his brave deeds, he raised his son to share the throne with him.

When Theseus saw the seven youths and girls going on board the black-sailed ship which was to take them to Crete, his daring imagination was fired in the midst of the general lamentation and he volunteered to go with the unfortunate contingent and to rescue them from danger. His father made him promise to set a white sail if he returned to Athens, to announce the happy outcome of the adventure.

In Crete, Theseus was the first man to leave the ship and he entered the palace of Minos before all the others. There Ariadne saw him and she fell in love with him at first sight. When The-

147

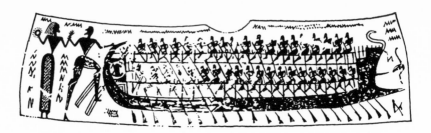

Theseus and Ariadne (with bridal wreath) boarding Athenian ship. Panorama from vase. Thebes

seus insisted on being the first again to be sent into the labyrinth, Ariadne gave him a ball of thread which he was to unwind as he entered the twisting passages, and which would then show him the way out of the maze again. It was Daedalus who gave Ariadne this ball of thread and she also gave Theseus her magic diadem which lit up in the darkness. Armed in this manner, Theseus appeared before the Minotaur and after a terrible duel he strangled the monster with his bare hands, and dragged the carcass out of the labyrinth by the horns.

By this act, the sinister power of Minos the Second was broken. Theseus set sail again with the fourteen young people he had saved, and Ariadne left Crete with them for Theseus intended to make her his queen in Athens. But on the island of Naxos, where they broke their journey, Dionysius put an end to their happiness. Minos had already promised Ariadne to the god and now he carried her off as she slept and to mark his triumph, he hurled her diadem into the sky where it has shone as a constellation ever since, lighting mariners on their way.

Theseus, beside himself with grief, forgot to hoist the white sail as they approached Athens. Aegeus, who was watching from the cliffs, saw the ship with its black sails, and overcome with anguish, he threw himself into the sea.

However, Theseus, the liberator, was received with great honor by the Athenians. The hero became a wise king, who made Athens powerful and gave the town an enduring code of laws.

For Minos, the age of power and happiness in Crete was over. Ariadne had left him, his son was dead too. And his mood grew so grim, it was as if Theseus had conquered him and not the Minotaur. He had Daedalus flung into a dungeon which had neither doors nor windows nor a roof. He intended that Daedalus should pay until the end of his days for the crime of giving Ariadne the ball of thread for Theseus.

But the cunning Daedalus made wings from feathers and wax for his son and himself, and with these they were able to rise out of the cell and escape across the sea. But only Daedalus managed to reach safety. Icarus, heedless of his father's warnings, rose high into the air and the wax which held the feathers together, melted in the heat of the sun and Icarus fell into the sea.

The King of Crete was so incensed at the escape of Daedalus, that he set out himself to track down the inventor. The king too thought out a plan. Among the many treasures he took with him, was a whorled shell and a thread. Wherever he went. he announced that he would heap with gold the man who could succeed in passing the thread through a tiny hole and along all the convolutions of the shell.

Eventually Minos arrived in Sicily where Cocalos was king. Cocalos said at once that he had at his court an artist who was more ingenious than any other. He gave the shell and the thread to Daedalus who had found refuge in his palace.

Daedalus knew immediately what to do. He tied one end of the thread to an ant, pushed it through the tiny hole into the shell, so that it crawled its way out again, drawing along the thread through all the spirals. When the ant appeared at the mouth of the shell, Daedalus showed his thanks by giving the insect its freedom once more and he handed the threaded shell to King Cocalos, who proudly took it to the Cretan King.

Minos was now certain that Daedalus was hiding in the palace of Cocalos and he demanded that the traitor be handed over for punishment. Cocalos promised to grant his guest's wish if he would give him a week's grace. But the Sicilian king had little inclination to give up the incomparable craftsman. He arranged a feast for Minos, and the daughter of Cocalos prepared a bath for the visitor. Prompted by Daedalus, she scalded the Cretan King to death, for the bathroom had concealed windows in the ceiling and Minos the Second came to a terrible end, as the princess and Daedalus poured cascades of boiling water over him. Daedalus showed his gratitude to Cocalos by creating new works of art for him the likes of which has never been seen before nor since.

Crete—A Book with a Thousand Seals

Theseus, the Greek hero, had vanquished the Minotaur in the labyrinth and freed the Athenians from the yoke of a cruel tribute. Daedalus, the Greek artist and inventor, had finally conquered Minos the Second. Thus ran the legend.

Troy too had been a legend. Agamemnon and Helen, Achilles and Odysseus were merely mythological figures—until Schliemann discovered the real Troy and found the bodies of real Achaeans in the royal graves of Mycenae. Had Theseus and Daedalus really lived too? Was it a fact that the early Greeks had come to Crete to shatter the power of Minos? Had they indeed triumphed over him, as described in the myths and by the Greek poets?

What is the position today? How much more have we learned since Evans uncovered the labyrinth, and many other eminent archaeologists have explored Crete, digging up finds by the thousands and making important discoveries?

This much can be stated as a fact: they have indeed come across the tracks of Theseus. They have found in Crete many things that are not Minoan at all but early Greek. And these include not only weapons, utensils, ornaments and jars, but also graves and buildings. So there must have been a time when the Achaeans settled on the island of Minos.

The final proof of this is found on those baked clay tablets with inscriptions on them. It is not the excavators but the philologists who have had the final say in the matter. And so in this chapter, there must be told the dramatic story of the decipherment of the Minoan script, at least in its broad outline.

It all began with the Cretan seals. Evans had gone to Crete in the first place because he expected to find there the key to those mysterious signs engraved on seals and signet rings. For years he had collected seals and impressions, wherever he could

possibly lay hands on them, and his collection included examples
from the simplest to the most precious. Then, when he discovered
the frescoes on which Minoans were portrayed, they showed
him that in ancient Crete, everyone wore a seal on the wrist
as a mark of identity—like an identification bracelet.

As the population of Crete increased rapidly at the time of
the Minoan palaces, thousands of new seals became necessary.
Obviously these seal impressions took the place of names in con-
tracts and letters, which explains their fantastic variety.

On these seals of agate or ivory, steatite, rock crystal, jasper,
carnelian, amethyst or some less precious stone, can be seen everything the Minoans encountered in their daily lives. And there are
thousands and thousands of them, no two of which are alike.
They show houses, heads, horns, plants and stars; tools of all

Minoan seal

kinds; birds, cats, scorpions and murex; monkeys and ibexes.
There are whole scenes too. For instance, an outrageously fat man
squats before a three-legged gaming table and moves a piece;
a fish brushes aside seaweed to deposit its eggs; three leafless
trees are lashed by the gale; dogs pounce on a stag; lions kill
bulls; demons appear with antlers on their backs, or with big
butterfly wings on their heads; a boxer knocks out his rival;
a bull jumper attempts the leap of death. Everything except
scenes of battle is to be found on these tiny seals. Together

they provided a picture book, but the text had still to be found.

The oldest Cretan seals date from about 2000 B.C. There are seal markings too covering both sides of a baked clay disk, which were brought to light in southern Crete from a stratum of the early sixteenth century B.C. For fifty years, this has been known as the Phaistos Disk, for it was found in Phaistos, the second largest of the Minoan palaces, where Italian archaeologists were digging at about the same time as Evans was in Knossos.

At the beginning of July 1908 Pernier, Halbherr's most famous colleague, came upon a rectangular storeroom. Here, on the evening of July 3, he chanced upon a broken tablet with writing on it, and immediately afterward, he found this round tablet which has a diameter of about six inches and is about one inch thick. On both sides there are sixty-one groups of pictures, clearly divided from one another and arranged in a spiral. The text uses forty-five different signs altogether, including human and animal heads, human figures, plants, birds, a jug, a disk with seven holes, a fish, flowers, and some more baffling symbols, which no one can identify for certain.

Since the disk was discovered, many people have tried to decipher it, one of the first of whom was Arthur Evans. In his opinion, the inscriptions began at the center, but if this were so it must have finished in a long wedge at the outer rim. This was wrong. On the contrary, near the rim on both sides there is a nick in the same place, just where the first "line" stops and the second begins. From this point, the text runs uninterrupted to the center. There were two further clues to the direction of the script. The figures would all be standing on their heads, if one started reading off from the center. And where two signs run into one another, the evidence is indisputable. The signs have been stamped or printed in the clay and where the "printer" has worked clumsily and damaged one sign with another, the blurred one must obviously be the earlier of the two. So the di-

The Phaistos Disc, front.

rection in which the writing runs is clear. It begins at the edge, like a phonograph record.

But what does the text mean? From various signs, Evans decided at first that it must be a paean of victory, and later he thought it must be a hymn. A German scholar named Ernst Sittig went to work more cautiously. For decades he had striven to solve the riddle of the Cretan script and he was well equipped to do so. At twenty three, he knew ten ancient and six modern languages. On Cyprus, he found a bi-lingual stone which had been cut in two. It was half in Greek and half in the language spoken in Cyprus in prehistoric times. During the First World War, Sittig gained vast experience in deciphering military codes. In 1950, he started anew to unravel the secret of the disk. He succeeded in interpreting the meaning of a number of the signs, but then death snatched him from his work.

Other notable scholars who also worked on the deciphering of the Cretan script remained basically unsuccessful. Only one thing

154

was clear. There had been three different and successive scripts in ancient Crete. The oldest was a picture writing like the hieroglyphs of the Egyptians. This was followed by a syllabic script that the experts called Linear A. From this Linear A had developed Linear B, the writing in which most of the clay tablets in the palace archives were inscribed.

Linear B tempted the scholars most, for most of the texts were written in it. Evans had discovered almost three thousand inscribed tablets in the palace of Knossos although it must be admitted, that by 1926, he had published only 120 of them. A great Finnish scholar, Sundwall, aroused Evans' displeasure when he copied thirty-eight of these tablets between 1932 and 1936 without permission, and because of this attitude, Evans was criticized, even by the two scholars who eventually managed to decipher the script. They wrote: "Two generations of scholars had been cheated of the opportunity to work constructively on the problem." Incidentally, they dedicated the work in which they published their eventual solution to Schliemann and not to Evans, although they were both Englishmen.

One of them was Michael Ventris. In 1936, when he was a fourteen year old schoolboy, he had heard Evans lecture in London. There cannot have been anyone in that lecture hall who listened with more absorbed attention. Four years later, as a student, Ventris published his first attempt at a solution, but he was on the wrong track. He thought the text of the disk was in one of the Etruscan languages, not a bad shot for an eighteen year old. Indeed eminent experts had held that the signs on Cretan sealings might be in any language and Hittite, Basque and Albanian were all seriously suggested.

During the half century 1901–1951 "continual attempts were made (to solve the problem) by reputable scholars, by talented amateurs and by cranks of all kinds from the lunatic fringe of archaeology." So wrote Ventris.

There was hardly one red herring that was not followed up. In 1927, Cowley, who was one of those jointly responsible for deciphering Hittite hieroglyphs, announced that he had deciphered six Cretan signs. Then Carl Blegen made another discovery, although this time it was on Greek soil and not in Crete. He found at Pylos a vast archive of clay tablets with the same script markings as those on the small tablets from Crete. Evans asserted at once that these tablets must have been carried off from Crete, or else they originated among Cretan emigrants who had founded a colony on the mainland of Greece.

The six hundred tablets from Pylos, the palace of the gray-haired Homeric hero Nestor, were carefully photographed and then buried away. The photographs were taken to the United States in the last American ship to leave the Mediterranean in 1940, where they were eventually published. An American mathematician and scientist, Alice Kober, who also had had a stab at trying to solve the mystery, finally acknowledged that it must be an unknown script in an unknown language. She gave

156

it up because "you can only get nothing from nothing." But she was mistaken. And it was she herself who took the first step "along an impossible path." It struck her that the same word reappeared in varying forms on the tablets, as if the nouns were declined, as for instance in the German *der Hund, des Hundes, dem Hunde,* or the Latin *servus, servum, servi, servo.* Therefore one must be dealing with what is known as an inflected language in which the different cases are distinguished by an alteration of the last syllable. That ruled out several languages from the start. For the first time, the field was narrowed, and the net closed in.

Alice Kober literally devised a 'net'—that is a screen or grid in whose spaces the words could be grouped according to a highly ingenious system. Ventris extended this 'grid' in several directions, so that more and more words were caught in his 'net'. Ventris was a professional architect who had been an airman during the war. Once he had examined the discoveries at Pylos, he abandoned the idea that the Cretan scripts had something to do with the Etruscan.

Between January 1951 and June 1952, he sent his interim findings to some twenty other scholars working on the problem and invited them to pull his theory to pieces. In 1952, at last through

Inscribed tablets;
left Linear A (older script); right Linear B. Knossos

a colleague of Evans, Sir John Myres, the second volume of Minoan inscriptions was published. The material for a basis of comparison was now considerably enlarged and more and more fish swam into the 'net' with which Ventris was working. Sometimes one 'fish' got caught in two or three interstices, where the meaning was still ambiguous. Then the architect Ventris found a collaborator in John Chadwick, a philologist. At eighteen, he had already learned Tibetan, Modern Greek and Sanskrit. During the war, he learned Japanese, 'in his spare time.' In 1946 he had hazarded a guess that Linear B might correspond to a form of very ancient Greek.

The collaboration of Ventris and Chadwick was extremely intensive and rewarding. Chadwick describes it in these words. "The break-through was due entirely to Ventris. But the actual definition of the words was only a beginning, and in the extremely laborious task of transposing the deciphered words into comprehensible Greek, we worked as equal partners, sent one another our suggestions and often, quite independently, hit upon the same ideas."

In the end, the method worked. By the subtle use of a statistical method, the network grew finer meshed and the different words began to emerge clearly.

In Linear B, the words are separated from each other by a dividing sign. Gradually twenty-eight symbols could be distinguished which come overwhelmingly on either side of the dividing lines, and therefore indicate either the beginnings or the ends of words. Through a vast number of detailed observations, it was confirmed that behind the signs there lay a form of Greek that was much more archaic than the Greek used in the *Iliad* and the *Odyssey*.

In 1952, Ventris and Chadwick published their discovery but it was not greeted by any means with unanimous approval. Even Blegen had misgivings. But when in the same year, another four hundred tablets were found at Pylos, and thanks to the key provided by Ventris and Chadwick these inscriptions could actually be read, they received general recognition.

This discovery has been hailed as one of the most important research achievements of our century. Ventris only survived his triumph by three years. At the age of thirty four, he was killed in a road accident.

Today, there is no doubt that Linear B developed from Linear A. As forty eight of the signs are common to both scripts, one can expect that Linear A will also be deciphered eventually. Today, we know too, that Linear scripts were in use from about 1700 B.C. until the fall of the Minoan palaces.

The signs of the older syllabic script are mainly scratched in stone and metal, engraved on gold rings or scribbled in ink on vases. Linear B has been preserved for the most part on clay tablets. No doubt it was written on leather and papyrus as well and one tradition has it that date palms on Crete were not planted principally for their fruit, but so that there would be enough writing 'leaves' for the use of government departments. Some of the inscriptions are so slapdash that they suggest the scribes were kept very busy.

After hundreds of tablets were deciphered, it could be seen that none of them contained the text of a story or poem, in short, no literature. Without exception, they dealt with sober facts, such as one finds in tax records or in bookkeeping. The entries are most precise. One unit of measurement seems to have been the sheep, which was very important for the Cretan economy, since it supplied meat, wool, milk and dung. There were also copper bars of fixed weight, poured into molds made of cattle hide. The taxpayers are entered by name; at the right edge of the tablet stands the amount paid. They calculated according to a decimal system very like ours, plus a simple form of fractions. Deliveries of corn and other goods are registered with much attention to detail. For instance, we have "imported white textiles with red borders—35." The pictogram for textile goods was the loom. There is a great deal about the Cretan economy to be learned from these entries. For instance, that wheat, barley and millet were cultivated and that the stock of olive trees was considerable. (Catchment grooves in the storerooms are another indication of the abundance of oil.) Saffron was sold by weight, honey in hollow measures whose capacity was shown according to the number of bees beside them. The size of the herds was truly astonishing. In one text, they mention twenty thousand sheep and seven hundred pigs. Armories also reveal their secrets, how many lances, arrows, swords, chariots and harnesses were stored in readiness. Occupations are listed too. There were doctors, bakers, coopers and goldsmiths; bowmakers, woodcutters, hunters, masons and bricklayers; cooks, oarsmen, shipwrights, blacksmiths and scribes; joiners, tailors, potters, dyers, fullers and carpenters.

The administration played a great role in the palace of Minos, but these records were never intended to last for all eternity. The signs were scratched on clay and the tablets dried in the open air, so that they fell to pieces in the course of time, unless they happened to be hardened by accident later when a palace was set on fire.

Linear B was, then, purely a palace script. No Minoan ever wore a seal with Linear B signs or markings. Apart from the palace scribes the early Cretans could not read this writing. It was the secret script of a language that was not native to the island, for it was in Greek.

Cretan writing,
scrawled in ink
inside a beaker

Opposite: The 'Harvesters' Vase', shaped
like an ostrich egg. Hagia Triada

Discoveries prove that this script was used in many palaces in Greece, that is, in all the citadels where the Achaean princes ruled. On Crete, they were found only in one palace, that of Knossos, and then only after 1500 B.C. or thereabouts. For this fact, there is only one explanation. The Achaeans must have been the masters of the kingdom of Minos from about that date. They who had long been vassals of the Cretan king, had put an end to the Minoan domination of the Aegean seas. One fine day, they overran the island and made themselves the masters in Cretan palaces. There are traces in Knossos to indicate that an earthquake came to their assistance, just as it had done at the siege of Troy. Evans found huge stones that had buried the house of a lamp maker beneath it, as they crashed down from the battlements of the palace wall.

From 1500 B.C. then, the sons of Minos were no longer the rulers of Crete and the Achaeans reigned in their stead. One of them was called Idomeneus and he set out with Agamemnon, Odysseus, Menelaus and Nestor for Troy. After 1500 B.C. the domed beehive graves of the Myceneans were erected in Crete. It is from this period onward, that the number of weapons found increases considerably.

In return, more Cretan craftsmen now came to the Greek mainland. In Tiryns and in other Mycenean fortresses, bull leaping was painted on the walls. On Mycenean gold cups, there appear representations of bulls as they were shown formerly only on Minoan vessels, beside trees that grow only in Crete.

Under the leadership of the Achaeans, all the Cretan palaces fell into ruin, with the exception of Knossos. Phaistos and Mallia which according to legend had been founded by the brothers of Minos, Phadamanthes and Sarpedon, had lost their meaning once foreigners were masters of the whole land and ruled it from one central point. The little islands off the north coast of Crete which had been famous during the Minoan period for the breeding of murex for purple dyes, became known as "the empty places."

With the invasion of the Achaeans, the Minoan civilization which had flourished for more than six hundred years, came to an end. The dainty dark-haired people whose grace, gaiety and daring captivate us from the many restored frescoes, were overcome by warriors from Mycenae, Thebes and Sparta. Theseus had conquered Minos.

The Secret of the Minotaur

After the conquest of the Minoan kingdom by the Achaeans, large numbers of Cretans left the island and migrated to the Cyclades, to Asia Minor and to Egypt. Their traces are to be found everywhere. They showed themselves capable of making new homes in widely scattered places and because they had so many skills at their command, they were welcomed everywhere. In Crete too, they went on producing many admirable works of art, there more than anywhere else.

The Achaean dominion of Crete lasted for a little less than a hundred years. Then the victors in their turn were overcome by the power that had so often devastated Crete, by the "bull" whose bellowing comes from inside the earth.

The Minoans had worshipped this power in statues of bulls and vessels shaped like bulls' heads. They had decorated their rooftops with pairs of horns and they had placed this sacred symbol in locations where they felt themselves closest to the divinity. The early Cretans were deeply aware of this constant threat to their existence, and such awareness found its most exciting expression in the "sacred sport," that is, leaping over the back of a charging bull. This stirring event is portrayed so often that we can imagine ourselves taking part in it too.

All around the great court in the Palace of Minos, the people of Knossos are assembled. Nobles and commoners have made their pilgrimage thither from the length and breadth of the island. There are so many of them that the stands cannot hold them all. They are in high festive mood, impatient for the display to come, which is to be performed before the eyes of the King and High Priest.

The tall young men and girls enter the ring. They carry no weapons. Then the bull is released and in he comes, confused by the noise and the smell of the crowds. One of the young men lures the bull toward him, provoking him to a frenzy. As the great beast rushes at the youth with its huge head lowered for the kill, the lad waits, motionless. At the decisive moment, however, he takes a flying leap into the air, seizing the horns that seek to destroy him, and using them as a hold, he sails over the back of the infuriated bull. This is repeated several times, as the other leapers in turn draw the bull towards them. But one of them misses his hold and the bull's horn gores deep into his breast. A stream of blood spurts forth, showing the place, and the thousands watching catch their breath. What has happened to this leaper can happen to any of them. Everyone is threatened at all times by the "bull" which not only strikes men down individually but which can destroy whole towns with such annihilating force that red streams gush from roofs and walls, and houses collapse to become burial mounds.

The game nears its end. The last leaper has vaulted over the bull. After so many forays, both its rage and its strength are exhausted. Now come the men with their nets and ropes. The bull is surrounded and finally captured. He is bound and dragged before the king, who raises the double ax and slays the beast. The blood of the sacrifice seeps into the lap of the earth, which is the Great Mother of us all. Life has conquered over the powers of destruction. As a sign of this triumph, the king places the sacred double ax on the head of the bull.

For many centuries, Crete was a seismic center, with at least three devastating earthquakes in each century. But even the worst disasters could not stop the Cretans from remaining within the danger zone. Time and again, after each devastation, they rebuilt their palaces and towns.

As these lines were being written, Nikolaus Platon was excavating a Minoan palace in Zakro, on the east coast of Crete. In this remote part of the island, Hogarth had already made finds which suggested that there must be greater deposits left, and quite recently, when a golden bull's head, a gold armlet, and a small golden dish were found at Zakro and brought to Platon, these finds prompted a large scale excavation made possible by the generosity of an American patron.

In the spring of 1964, Platon was able to announce that he had come upon the ruins of a palace. Zakro had never been looted and so, in their very first season, the excavators were able to dig up many wonderful vessels of earthenware and stone, double axes and pairs of horns. Among their earliest finds were four elephant tusks and the capital of a pillar of black stone, which shows that Evans made no mistake in guessing the shape of such columns for the restoration of the Palace of Knossos. Another discovery of major importance was a collection of about five hundred seal impressions and of fourteen small tablets with pictogram inscriptions.

The fate of the palace of Zakro must have been decided in a matter of minutes by violent earth tremors. The horror-stricken residents tried to run out into the open, that is, all who had not been crushed to death immediately beneath the collapsing walls. In the flicker of an eyelid, the whole palace went up in flames, fed lavishly by the abundant stores of oil. This catastrophe left behind it a feeling of such aversion, that Zakro had been shunned by the Cretans for more than three thousand years.

We know the exact year when the Palace of Knossos was finally destroyed. It was in 1425 B.C. when a strong wind from the south fanned the flames along the burning joists set horizontally into the walls. That was ascertained from the ruins themselves by Pendlebury, a major British archaeologist, who lived on the site for many years and who knew the Palace of Knossos inside out. He was killed fighting in Crete during the last war. This is what he wrote: "The Throne Room . . . was found in a state of complete confusion. A great oil jar lay overturned in one corner, ritual vessels were in the act of being used when the disaster came. It looks as if the king had been hurried there to undergo some last ceremony, in the hopes of saving the people."

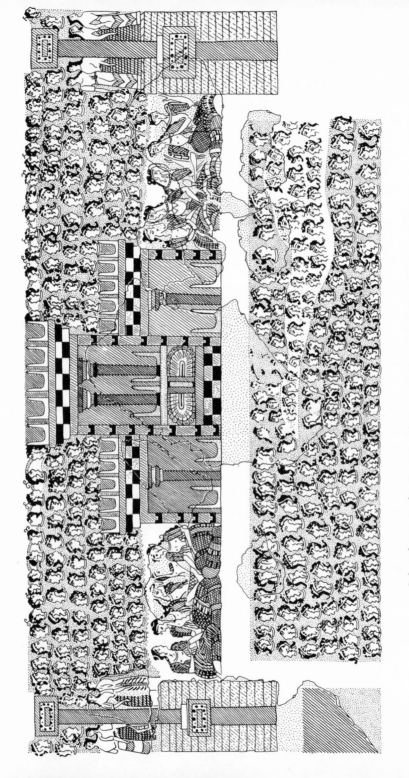

Cult gathering in the Great Court. Fresco. In the center is the 'chapel royal'. Knossos

It was too late. Without warning, the "bull within the earth" had struck its most violent, annihilating blow. The double ax was shattered forever. A wondrous building was transformed into a smoking heap of rubble. In the tempest of fire, the inscribed clay tablets in the archives were baked hard into lasting documents. We have an instance from the last century of what can happen to an island when an earthquake and a volcanic eruption take place simultaneously.

On August 6 and 7, 1883, a volcano erupted on the island of Krakatoa in the Dutch East Indies. Within minutes, the towns of Telog and Tyazingin were completely destroyed. The sinister rumbling could be heard over a sixth of the earth's surface. Houses collapsed in a radius of four hundred ninety-two miles. The ash that was thrown up changed noon into night and about a thousand miles away, a rain of ashes fell. A fine veil of ashes was carried right around the globe. Tidal waves fifty feet high flattened whole villages, railways were obliterated, forests devastated, and ships were carried inland for miles. Fires broke out as lamps were overturned and hearths were damaged.

There were 36,417 people killed.

Three thousand three hundred years earlier, a comparable catastrophe took place in the Aegean Sea but it must have been about four times as violent, to judge from the relative size of the two volcanic craters. This was the eruption that destroyed the Palace of Minos for good, and it was then too that three-quarters of the Island of Thera (Santorin) was blown sky high. Thera is sixty eight miles from Crete. With an eruption four times as powerful and the much deeper sea, the tidal waves must have been twice as high as at the Krakatoa disaster. Within minutes the coastal settlements and the harbors were destroyed and even villages in the interior were laid waste. High in the mountains passages to the grottoes caved in.

At that moment, the horror-stricken Cretans must have lost their faith in every protecting godhead. Of the Island of Thera,

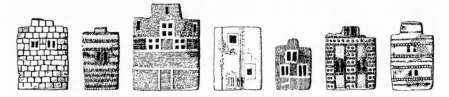

Minoan houses. Faience tablets
up to 2" high. Knossos

once circular in shape, only a crescent remained above sea level and this was buried under a layer of volcanic ash and lava nearly one hundred feet thick in places. At the same moment, the palace of King Minos in Crete was reduced to a heap of rubble.

Twice did Evans himself have this uncanny experience of earth-shattering powers at work. The first time was on April 20, 1922 at fifteen minutes past noon, when the workmen were busy clearing out a ruined cellar. In each corner there was a bull's skull, obviously the remains of animals that had been sacrificed. Then "a short sharp shock, sufficient to throw one of my men backward, accompanied by a deep rumbling sound was experienced on the site, and throughout the entire region."

A far more violent tremor occurred four years later in 1926. Evans described the experience for us in an impressive passage. ". . . On June 26 . . . at 9:45 in the evening of a calm warm day, the shocks began. They caught me reading on my bed in the basement room of the headquarters house, and trusting to the exceptional strength of the fabric, I chose to see the earthquake through from within. Perhaps I had hardly realized the full awesomeness of the experience, though my confidence in the full strength of the building proved justified, since it did not suffer more than slight cracks. But it creaked and groaned, and rocked from side to side, as if the whole must collapse . . . The movement, which recalled a ship in a storm, though of only a minute and a quarter's duration, already produced the same effect of

Opposite: Minoan cup, with sculptured flowerheads. Phiastos

sickness on me as a rough sea. A dull sound rose from the ground, like the muffled roar of an angry bull. . . As the quickly re- peated shocks produced their cumulative effect, the crashing of the roofs of the two small houses outside the garden gate made themselves audible, mingled with women's shrieks and the cries of some small children. . . Meanwhile a mist of dust, lifted up- wards by a sudden draught of air, rose sky high, so as almost en- tirely to eclipse the full moon, some house lights reflected on this dark bank, giving the appearance of a conflagration wrapped round with smoke. . .

"The archeological *sequitur* of this is very important. When, as in the great Palace of Knossos, we find evidence of a series of overthrows, some of them on a scale that could hardly be the work of man, there seems real reason for tracing the cause to the same seismic agencies. . .

"It is something to have heard with one's own ears the bellow- ing of the bull beneath the earth who, according to a primitive belief, tosses it on his horns. It was doubtless the constant need of protection against these petulant bursts of the infernal powers that explains the Minoan tendency to concentrate their worship on the chthonic aspect of their great goddess, wreathed with serpents as Lady of the Underworld."

Never again was the excavator of the Palace of Minos so near to Ancient Crete as in that hour when he heard the bull bellow- ing within the earth.

This bull the Achaeans came to know in all its monstrous vio- lence on two occasions. First as their allies when they attacked the kingdom of Minos and then as the enemy one hundred years later, when it turned against the conquerors, this time to destroy them.

They themselves had another mythical picture for the same destructive force—the horses of Poseidon whose hoofbeats had shattered the walls of Troy.

So we are confronted by an astonishing coincidence. After the excavations of Schliemann and Evans, Dörpfeld and Pendlebury, Halbherr and Pernier, Hazzidakis and Platon, Fabricius, Hogarth, Karo and a hundred others, we learn that Troy and Knossos were destroyed in virtually identical fashion. The last rulers of the Palace of Minos were Achaeans like Odysseus of Ithaca and Nestor of Pylos. It was brother fighting brother with Agamemnon and Priam, both of whose ancestors had come from the lands of the Danube.

The archaeologists have proved that the myths are not the free inventions of ancient poets. And the research of Ventris and Chadwick give us reason to hope that Evans' dream of deciphering both the signs on Cretan seals and the mysterious disk of Phaistos will be realized in the foreseeable future.

In ten decades of intensive excavation, so much valuable and conclusive information has come to light that the wheel has come full circle. The great ring is closed with its three gems, the stones of Troy, Mycenae, and Knossos.

Ancient Cretan picture writing

The Ring of Minos

Evans had spent a "whole lifetime" digging in Knossos. As at Troy, stratum after stratum had emerged from the hill of Kephala, palace had been built upon palace.

It was even harder for Evans to keep these strata separate than it had been for Schliemann, for the Cretan palaces were not built of Cyclopean walls. There was literally nothing left standing of most of the flimsy walls of gypsum and it would have been impossible to reassemble their widely scattered fragments in order to reconstruct them. Evans, backed by his architects, led a stubborn fight to show the world the palace as it once had been, but one must admit that in spite of all his efforts, most of it was beyond rescue.

Of the great house with its terraces and stairways, the two uppermost flights had vanished almost completely. This Evans had to accept when he uncovered the terraces with the assistance of Greek miners. They found the charred remains of the old wooden pillars that had once supported the roof. Part of one wall was still standing but it was leaning dangerously and liable to collapse at any moment. Evans had it "harnessed and secured by planks and ropes; its base was then cut into, along the whole length; on either side, wedge-shaped stones and cement being held in readiness for insertion in the outer slit, and sixty men on the terrace above were then set to pull the ropes secured to the casing. The mighty mass was thus set in motion and righted itself against the solid wooden framework prepared as a stop. This was then removed and the whole structure refixed in its upright position."

Such operations were necessary at every step and turn and in the many volumes of his "Palace of Minos," Evans describes dramatic incidents like this. He tells too how at last he brought himself to use materials for the restoration which had not even been known when the labyrinth was built.

The supporting timbers, props, and wooden posts with which he tried to manage at first were only makeshift at best. There was danger that the whole building might collapse, for the remains of the upper floors were threatening to cave in on top of the lower ones and bury everything beneath them.

The architect, Christian Doll, struggled heroically with the task. Iron girders were shipped from England at great cost, since cypress beams, which had served as supports in Minos' day were no longer obtainable, and pine trunks imported from the Tyrol had proved unsuitable for the changeable Cretan climate, as they learned from experience elsewhere.

From the nineteen twenties on, Evans used concrete for reinforcement, in spite of the fact that it brought him many reproaches.

All in all, Evans worked for half a century on behalf of Knossos. He was a man who liked to take his time, and he was never in a hurry, even to publish his experiences as an excavator. When at eighty years of age, he paid a visit to Dalmatia and saw once again the prison in Ragusa where he had been locked up as a revolutionary, he told the warden, "I come back every fifty years." It was by a good fifty years, too, that he survived the man who had dug up Troy and Mycenae.

Like Schliemann, Evans had great financial means at his disposal and again like Schliemann, he used them without thought of self. In addition, though, Evans had had an excellent education, and so he was better equipped for his work than the pastor's son from Ankershagen.

His vision was more reliable too. The number of his personal finds runs into tens of thousands and many of his judgments are still valid today. Furthermore, his division of the Minoan centuries into three great epochs has never yet been set aside. It was only his prime object, the deciphering of the Cretan script, that was denied him. This does not take away from his greatness any more than it detracts from Schliemann's glory that he was mistaken in thinking the Trojan gold he found was the Treasure of Priam, or that he believed the finest of the Mycenean gold masks had covered the face of Agamemnon.

Wherever a world formerly unknown is opened up, errors are unavoidable. And often these errors in themselves provide a clue to unraveling profound secrets. Evans was eighty years old when he pulled off his last exciting triumph and it was triggered off by a forgery which at first he failed to detect as such.

The scene of the discovery lies less than a mile to the south of the Palace of Minos, in a region where hitherto no Minoan remains of any kind had come to light. In 1932 a stranger offered Evans a large gold ring, "the Ring of Minos." It was bigger than any gold ring they had found so far and a magnificent piece of work. But the man who was trying to sell the ring, demanded a sum that even Evans found very high.

The old scholar photographed the ring first of all, so that he could study it more closely in print. The stranger told him that the children of the village priest had found the ring while playing, and that the priest would not sell it to anyone but the excavator of Knossos. He even showed Evans the spot where the ring had been found.

When Evans had examined the photograph thoroughly, he went to the priest to buy the "Ring of Minos," convinced that he had come upon a unique find which was worth the high price asked for it. But now the priest declared in dismay that the stranger had vanished with the ring, no one knew where. All their inquiries led nowhere.

Then Evans did something that seemed to be entirely irrational. Although he was now certain that he had had dealings with an exceptionally accomplished forger, whose statements about the place where the ring had been found were totally unreliable, Evans began to dig on that most unpromising spot. And he came upon the grave vault of a Minoan prince, which was finer than any of the rock graves hitherto discovered.

The Palace of Knossos. Reconstruction of west wing,
with stairway to main floor and 'chapel royal' (cf. ill. p. 166)

The vault had been dug deep in the rock and the floor and the walls were lined with alabaster slabs. An alabaster pillar had once carried a strong crossbeam to support the roof of rock.

The ceiling had been painted blue so that the dead man could have the color of the sky above him. Near the grave chamber, was a cult room with two pillars similar to those in the chamber by the Throne Room in the Palace of Minos.

Above this little chamber there was a larger hall with several columns. The lower cult room, through which the coffin had been taken into the burial vault was locked from within. As "the dead man could not have locked himself in," to quote one of those present at the discovery, there must have been a trap door in the ceiling through which the coffin bearers could climb out into the upper hall, for an earthquake had brought down the roof and there was only one skeleton in the rock grave.

And so Evans, following the trail of the forged "Ring of Minos" had come upon "The Grave of Minos." Finder's luck was faithful to him to the end.

It had eluded Schliemann when he had tried to conquer the realm of Minos for himself. The man who excavated Troy and Mycenae never knew that among the objects he himself had brought to light were many of Minoan origin.

Among the finds from the shaft graves of Mycenae, there is a dagger which displays no lions either hunting or hunted, but "a stretch of the Nile". Fish swim placidly through the water, but a desperate hunt is going on in a clump of papyrus above, with leopards stalking wild ducks. A few manage to fly away, but none of the leopards go away with empty paws and one of them has even managed to 'bag' two ducks. The robbers and their feathered prey are captured forever in the gold and silver of the dagger. It is a work of art that reminds one of the pictures in Amarna and Knossos. No wonder. A Cretan craftsman made it.

Schliemann who found this "Nile Dagger" never saw the Minoan frescoes. They were buried under a layer of oxide which was removed only after Schliemann's death. He did not realize the implications of many of his own finds, just as Evans misinterpreted many things. Such errors they share with Columbus, who obstinately insisted that he had found the western passage to the Indies and not a new continent. That does not detract from the greatness of his deed. Even if America is called after Amerigo Vespucci and not after Columbus, he remains the real discoverer of America. It is the same with Schliemann and Evans. The work of both men was too enormous for them to be able to satisfy themselves on every little detail. Through them a start was made in Troy, in Mycenae and Knossos, and their contribution to archaeology remains supreme.

Other eminent excavators and scholars have continued their work, so that we today have a clear picture of those early civilizations that concern us more closely than any others. For the achievements of the Mycenean-Minoan cultures exerted their influence on Greece and Rome, and through them on ours today. It was in Crete and Mycenae that western civilization began.

On the coast where Troy was built, also stood the palace of King Agenor, whose beautiful daughter was carried away across the sea by Zeus, disguised as a splendid bull. Agenor sent out his sons to seek the kidnapped girl and bring her back. But they in their turn never returned home either. Wherever they went, the sons of Agenor built cities and fortresses for their sister Europa. In other words, they laid the foundations of Europe.

From the excavations of Troy, Mycenae and Crete, we know that this is not a myth but a true account.

Vase with octopus. 11" high. Crete

Glossary of Proper Names and Terms Used

Achaeans
: Migrants from the Danube basin who established the Mycenean culture in Greece

Achilles
: Achaean hero of the *Iliad*

Acropolis
: Hilltop town and fortress in ancient Greek cities

Aegean Sea
: The Greek Sea, eastern part of the Mediterranean

Aegisthus
: Son of Thyestes who, in league with Clytemnestra, murdered Agamemnon on his return from Troy

Agamemnon
: King of Mycenae "Prince of Men," who led the Achaean expedition against Troy

Agate
: Semi-precious stone

Agenor
: King of Tyre, father of Europa, who bore three sons to Zeus on the island of Crete-Minos, Rhadamanthus and Sarpedon

Agora
: Open space where the inhabitants of ancient Greek cities gathered on all important occasions

Alabaster
: Soft, translucent stone, much used for ornamental vessels and for lining walls

Amarna art
: Egyptian art at the time of the Pharaoh Ikhnaton (14th century B.C.) who repudiated the numerous traditional gods and believed in one divinity for all mankind. Many Cretan craftsmen were employed in the palace that he built

Amethyst
: Semi-precious stone

Antelion
: Small, highly dangerous, venomous snake, with which the hill of Hissarlik was swarming

Apollo
: Greek god of light and of the sciences

Argos
: Mycenean city and province. Homer calls it "Argos where the horses graze"

Ariadne
: Minos' daughter, who gave the Athenian hero Theseus a ball of thread so that he could find his way out of the labyrinth after he had conquered the Minotaur

Artemis
: Greek goddess, sister of Apollo

Atreus
: King of Mycenae, founder of the accursed dynasty that included Agamemnon and Orestes

Bunarbashi
: Village and hill in the plain of Troy, considered by many people to be the site of Homer's Troy.

Byblos
: Important Phoenician port

177

Carnelian	(Also spelled 'cornelian') Red semi-precious stone, suitable for engraving
Casemate(s)	Fortification wall(s) containing vaulted chambers
Cassandra	Trojan prophetess, Agamemnon's prize of war, murdered with him on his return from Troy
Catalhüyük	Cult center in Asia Minor where evidence of bull worship was discovered dating from 6th millenium B.C.
Chian	Pharaoh of Hyksos epoch (after 1700 B.C.)
Chthonic	Dwelling in or beneath the surface of the earth, implying divine creative force and fertility
Colchis	Village on the Black Sea coast. When Agamemnon was about to sacrifice his daughter Iphigenia, Artemis spirited her away to Colchis in a cloud.
Cuirass	Breastplate, armored corselet
Curetes	Spirits of the earth, entrusted with the care of the new-born Zeus
Cyclops	Race of giants in Greek mythology, builders of Tiryns and other 'Cyclopean' fortresses
Delos	Granite island, birthplace of Apollo
Delphi	Location of the oracle of Apollo
Dionysius	Greek god of wine and fertility, who abducted Ariadne when she and Theseus were running away from Crete
Diorite	Granulated and variegated stone, much used for vessels and statues
Etruscans	Ancient Italian race of pre-Roman times
Faience	Decorated pottery with an impermeable glaze
Firman	Official permit issued by the Turkish government
Fresco	Paintings on walls, carried out with casein pigments while the plaster is still damp
Gortyn	Ancient town in central Crete, where an early Greek wall inscription was discovered
Granulation	Goldsmith's technique for soldering tiny gold and silver beads to the surface of jewelry, etc., for ornamentation
Hector	Son of Trojan King Priam, killed fighting against Achilles, who dragged him around the city of Troy
Helen	Wife of Spartan King Menelaus, carried off by Trojan Prince Paris and brought back to Greece by the Achaeans after a ten year war
Helladic	Bronze Age civilization on the Greek mainland
Hera	Wife of Zeus
Hercules	Model for all Greek heroes, born in Tiryns and granted immortality for performing great deeds
Hesiod	The most important poet after Homer, of pre-classical Greece. Of Boeotian peasant extraction, born c.700 B.C.

178

Hittites	Indo-Germanic race who founded an empire in the Near East in the second millenium B.C. and destroyed Troy II c.1900 B.C.
Hissarlik	Turkish word for "small fortress"; the mound in which Schliemann discovered the city of Troy
Homer	Poet, author of the *Iliad* and the *Odyssey;* supposed to have lived before 700 B.C.
Hyksos	Warlike peoples from Asia Minor, who ruled Egypt between 1700 and 1500 B.C.
Ikhnaton	The Pharaoh Amenophis IV, founder of the Amarna culture
Iliad	One of Homer's two great epics, telling the story of the Trojan War in poetry
Jasper	Semi-precious stone, can be yellow, red, or brown
Keftiu	Ancient Egyptian name for the Cretans
Kephala	"Squires' Knoll," the mound from which Arthur Evans excavated the Palace of Minos
Labyrinth	"House of the Double Ax," the Palace of Minos at Knossos; but according to later Greek versions of the Theseus legend, a subterranean maze, home of the Minotaur, a monster who ate human flesh
Laomedon	The king for whom Poseidon built the city of Troy
Lapis lazuli	Blue semi-precious stone
Mari	The ruins of a kingdom on the middle Euphrates dating from the 3rd to the 2nd millenium B.C.; discovered in 1933, notable chiefly for a large collection of cuneiform archives.
Megaron	"The King's Hall," rectangular in shape, with ante-room and main hall and central, circular hearth place. Introduced by migrants from the north into Greece. The Greek temple is a development of the megaron
Minos	Son of Zeus and Europa, the first king of Crete
Minotaur	"The Bull of Minos," a monster half man, half bull, to whom the tyrant Minos fed human flesh, according to later Greek legends
Mycenae	Palace of the Achaeans in the Peloponnese
Nausicaa	Princess, who found Odysseus when he was shipwrecked on the Island of the Phaeacians (Schliemann believed Phaeacia was Corfu)
Naxos	Greek island, where Dionysius abducted Ariadne
Obsidian	Dark vitreous lava or volcanic rock, like bottle glass
Odyssey	Homer's epic poem, describing the adventures of Odysseus during his ten years of wandering from Troy to Ithaca
Olympus	Place sacred to the ancient Greeks, where games were held every four years in honor of the gods

179

Olympiad	The sacred games, which date back to 776 B.C. During the games, all quarrels and feuds were forbidden
Orchomenos	Achaean royal residence, like Mycenae "rich in gold," according to Homer
Osiris	Ancient Egyptian god, murdered by his brother Seth and resurrected when his sister Isis found him again after a long search
Ovid	Roman poet (43 B.C.–18 A.D.)
Paidos	"Time to stop work", Turkish word of uncertain derivation
Papyrus	Reed which grows by the Nile, manufactured by the ancient Egyptians into 'paper'.
Paris	Trojan prince who, prompted by Aphrodite, carried off the beautiful Helen
Paros	Greek island famous for its marble
Patroclus	Friend of Achilles, slain by Hector
Pelasgian Wall	Remains of Mycenean citadel on the Acropolis of Athens
Pericles	Leading statesman of Athens (c.499–429 B.C.) contemporary of the poets Aeschylus, Sophocles and Euripides, the historians Herodotus and Thucydides, the philosopher Socrates and many important artists
Phaeacians	Island people mentioned by Homer, who welcomed Odysseus at the end of his ten-year wanderings
Pharaoh	The Great House, title of the kings of ancient Egypt
Pithos (-oi)	Tall earthenware storage jar(s)
Plato	Greek philosopher (427–347 B.C.)
Priam	King of Troy at the time of the war commemorated by Homer
Propyleum (a)	Grand entrance to an acropolis, the space between the "sacred and profane"
Psychro	Cult shrine to the east of the Lasithi plateau in Crete
Pylos	"Sandy Pylos", palace of the gray-haired Nestor who went to war against Troy with Agamemnon
Rhadmanthus	Brother of Minos, ruler of Phaistos, Crete, made king of the underworld, because he was so just
Rhea	Mother of Zeus
Rhyton	Drinking cup, often in the form of an animal's head
Santorin(i)	Also known as Thera, Greek volcanic island where Schliemann was once shipwrecked
Sarpedon	Brother of Minos, ruler of Mallia, Crete
Sinter	Deposit oozing from damp cave walls to form a coating over cave paintings and votive gifts
Sistrum	Ancient Egyptian musical instrument, like a rattle
Steatite	"Soapstone," soft mineral, usually dark green, used for making jars etc.

Stele	Stone slab set up in a public place; also a gravestone
Talus	Sloping mass of fragments at base of cliff or wall
Tauros	Legendary giant of brass, said to guard the coasts of Crete
Thera	(also known as Santorin). Greek island which was reduced to one-third of its former size by a volcanic eruption c.1500 B.C. which also destroyed Minoan palaces in Crete
Theseus	Athenian prince who conquered the Minotaur
Tholos	Underground tomb shaped like a beehive
Thucydides	Greek historian, military strategist and naval commander (460–403 B.C.)
Troad	Province bordering on the Dardanelles with Troy as its capital
Tyre	Phoenician capital, palace of King Agenor, father of Europa
Ugarit	Ancient kingdom of Asia Minor
Yam(k)had	Ancient kingdom of Asia Minor
Zeus	Father of the gods for the ancient Greeks

Chronological Table
(according to Marinatos and Karo)

Pre 2600 B.C. Neolithic age in Crete

2600–2000 Early Minoan culture; harbors in eastern Crete; earliest seals; round graves

until 2500 Neolithic age (Sesklo culture) in Greece; settlement of Greece by communities from Asia Minor

2500–2300 Neolithic age (Dimini culture) overlapping with Bronze Age in Greece

pre 2500 Troy I, pirate stronghold, some trading

2500–1900 Early Helladic culture; from 2000 onward, infiltration by Achaeans from Danube basin

2400–1900 Troy II, monarchy of growing importance

2000–1580 Middle Minoan culture (I–IIIa) earliest palaces, Kamares ceramics, oldest picture writing; followed by heyday of palaces and paintings; many mansions; towns; extensive trade

c. 1900 Troy II destroyed by Hittites

1900–1500 Troy III–V, reduced to provincial significance

1900–1580 Middle Helladic culture in Greece

c. 1700 Old palaces of Crete destroyed by earthquake

from 1650 Building of Mycenean citadels

1600–1500 Early Mycenean culture; shaft graves

1580–1500 Middle Minoan culture (IIIb); change of style in painting and pottery

after 1550 Destruction of Cretan palaces by earthquakes

1550–1425 Achaean domination of Crete and the Aegean; archives in Palace of Knossos in Linear B script, as in the archives of Mycenean citadels

1500–1400 Late Minoan culture; high water mark of last epoch

1500–1280 Troy VI, powerful kingdom

1500–1100 Late Helladic culture, beehive graves, archives; c. 1150, destruction of Mycenean citadels

1425 Palace of Knossos finally destroyed by exceptionally severe earthquake and tidal wave combined, along with a volcanic eruption on Santorin (Thera)

c. 1280 Troy VI destroyed by earthquake and act of war (after the siege described by Homer)

until 1250 Crete dominated by the Achaeans; Idomeneus, King of Crete and "descendant of Minos" takes part in the Trojan campaign (according to Homer)

c. 1250	Troy rebuilt (Troy VII)
after 1200	Beginning of Dorian migration; tribes from northern Greece press southward; Mycenean citadels strengthened
pre 1100	Dorians, having founded the Greek city states, invade Crete

ACKNOWLEDGMENTS FOR COLOR PLATES

Burges, Grosshesselohe (*Uni-Dia-Verlag*): facing pp. 16, 17, 48, 65, 96, 128, 129, 144 (bottom)

Hirmer, Munich: facing pp. 32, 33, 49 (top), 64

J. J. *Knoch*, Khora Sfakion, Crete: facing pp. 80, 81, 144 (top), 145, 169

J. A. *Lavaud*, Paris (*Holle-Archive*): facing pp. 49 (bottom), Jacket

N. *Platon*, Athens: facing pp. 97, 120 (and following page), 121 (and preceding page), 160, 168

Also by Hans Baumann
The Caves of the Great Hunters
The World of the Pharaohs
Gold and Gods of Peru